Jon Harris

Jon is a Director of Accounting4Actors Ltd, a private specialist accountancy practice for creative industry professionals. He is a fully-qualified Chartered Management Accountant. He is a graduate of Cambridge University and holds a Masters in Organisational Psychology from the Tavistock Centre.

He started his career in the arts, first as a director, then producing and managing the finances of theatre shows in the West End and on tour all over the world. He was Producer at Shared Experience and was the founding Director of Stratford Circus arts centre.

He is a qualified Adult Education teacher, and was an Associate Tutor at Goldsmiths' University Institute for Creative and Cultural Entrepreneurship.

He is a Fellow of the RSA and a Trustee and Treasurer of Disability Arts Online.

He spends most days in a state of abject misery about either golf, Chelsea Football Club, or both.

THE COMPACT GUIDES

are pocket-sized introductions for actors and theatremakers, each tackling a key topic in a clear and comprehensive way. Written by industry professionals with extensive hands-on experience of their subject, they provide you with maximum information in minimum time.

Published titles include:

BREAKING DOWN YOUR SCRIPT
Laura Wayth

GETTING INTO DRAMA SCHOOL
Nick Moseley

**GETTING, KEEPING & WORKING
WITH YOUR ACTING AGENT**
JBR

DEVELOPING YOUR EMOTIONAL HEALTH
Andy Barker, Brian Cooley & Beth Wood

LEARNING YOUR LINES
Mark Channon

MAKING YOUR SOLO SHOW
Lisa Carroll & Milly Thomas

MANAGING YOUR MONEY
Jon Harris

MASTERING AN AMERICAN ACCENT
Rebecca Gausnell

The publisher welcomes suggestions
for future titles in the series.

MANAGING YOUR MONEY
THE COMPACT GUIDE

Jon Harris

NICK HERN BOOKS
London
www.nickhernbooks.co.uk

A Nick Hern Book

Managing Your Money: The Compact Guide
first published in Great Britain in 2026
by Nick Hern Books Limited, The Glasshouse,
49a Goldhawk Road, London W12 8QP

Copyright © 2026 Jon Harris

Jon Harris has asserted his moral right to be identified
as the author of this work

Designed and typeset by Nick Hern Books, London
Printed and bound in the UK by Clays Ltd,
Elcograf S.p.A.

A CIP catalogue record for this book
is available from the British Library

ISBN 978 1 84842 552 3

www.nickhernbooks.co.uk/environmental-policy

Nick Hern Books' authorised representative in the EU is
Easy Access System Europe – Mustamäe tee 50, 10621 Tallinn, Estonia
email gpsr.requests@easproject.com

Contents

Introduction		7
1.	Budgeting	15
2.	Tax Basics and Getting Started	21
3.	Income and Preparing for Tax	41
4.	Tax and Expenses	77
5.	Pensions, Mortgages, Savings, Insurance and Benefits	133
6.	VAT and Limited Companies	167
7.	Producing Your Own Work	203
Appendices		
	Alex's Career Finance Checklist	223
	Glossary	226
	Abbreviations	233
Acknowledgements		235

Introduction

Our objectives

I think some readers will take to this book like ducks to water. Everything will make sense, every piece of the money jigsaw will fall effortlessly into place, you will sail into your own budgets and tax returns with hardly a look back, and you will laugh at all my jokes knowingly.

But others will hate this subject, this book, me, the publishers, HMRC, the Pharoah who first collected tax in about 3000 BC (I owe him a beer, actually) and absolutely anything connected to this wretched topic. You hate numbers, you will read things I've written and scream 'BUTWHYYYYY???', and you'll send me furious emails.

And if you are in the second of these groups – well – sorry. I know that the mere mention of this kind of thing makes you want to bury your head in the nearest bucket. And I sympathise. But I also want to help you, and you're here now, right? So sigh deeply, settle down, accept that everyone's got to do it, and off we go.

This book is a compact guide, but that belies the size of this huge topic. This book can only serve as an introduction, to point you in the right direction and to help you to focus on what matters, and avoid any obvious pitfalls.

This book:

- Outlines the key considerations regarding personal finance and tax management which all creative industry workers in the UK should consider. You'll find it most useful if you are embarking on your creative career. I'm mindful, when I say 'embarking on your creative career', that only some people do that when they are young; and only some people intend to do it full-time. I also very much have in mind those who may be starting a creative journey later in life, and very possibly alongside other professional and family commitments.

- Also helps experienced, full-time, seasoned pros. It's never too late to reform bad habits and start good ones, and so experienced creatives will benefit from this book too.

- Provides a checklist to help you ensure that you have covered all bases.

- Points you towards more resources and help in various areas.

- Shows you how to look out for the milestones in your career which may signal to you that you should look for more help and resources than you may have needed in the past.

- Ends with a helpful glossary for all those technical terms you might encounter – out in the world, or while reading this book. Words which are glossed are greyscale the first time they appear here.

A short disclaimer

I don't want to spend the whole book reminding you of what we *cannot* do here, so here's a short disclaimer that applies to the whole topic; let's acknowledge it, and then leave it to one side and go on.

All the financial and tax advice the book gives is couched in general terms; it describes common situations and points to broad questions and answers. Everyone's individual detailed circumstances are different. The book can help point you in the right direction, but it isn't a substitute for detailed financial and tax consideration of your personal changing situation from year to year. Almost anybody is likely to receive a higher quality of financial and tax advice if they consult a suitably qualified and experienced professional about their own circumstances, rather than trying to get everything 100% right using only published sources. You are no different.

Furthermore, although we would all hope for a UK finance and tax system that is entirely, objectively clear on every point, we don't have one, and neither does any other country in the world. Therefore some of the content of this book represents simply my subjective opinion. Another accountant might tell you something different to what I have written here about x or y.

That said, remember that the creative industries are a niche field, and the day-to-day activities and concerns of those who work in them are generally not well understood by people who have not worked in them. Most qualified accountants are perfectly competent at giving advice to, say, delivery drivers and plumbers. But I myself would not accept, say, a vet, a tree-surgeon or an oil-rig mechanic as a client. Not knowing anything at all about those industries other than what a normal consumer knows, I cannot really conceive enough about the activities, dilemmas and pressures in those peoples' working lives to give them very good tax advice about their businesses.

Similarly, I advise you to be very wary of financial and tax advice given to you by accountants, even qualified ones, if they are not *specialists in the creative industries*. There are too many unusual corners, idiosyncrasies, doubts, ifs and buts about the financial life of a creative industry worker. The vast majority of accountants simply do not understand these, and I have observed frequently that this lack of knowledge leads them to judgements which do not amount to the best financial advice for you, in most cases.

I use the word 'actor' quite often in this book as a shorthand for 'anyone working in theatre, film, TV and/or other entertainment media'. If you are a writer, director, stage manager, designer, producer, etc., please excuse the shorthand – the great majority of what is discussed here is also relevant to you. Many people will be doing more than one creative thing; acting as well as writing, for example; and there will sometimes be particular matters that only apply to one type of work. For example, actors will generally be able to deduct the cost of their haircuts from their pre-tax income, and writers generally will not. So I have tried to focus on the matters which are common ground to all creative work, and you will need to read all this advice through the lens of your own particular activities and situation, especially if you have a hyphen in your job title.

I discuss various types of financial products or accounts in this book, and I mention several times that these can be bought or opened via comparison websites. I do not recommend any particular website nor any particular product or account. You should carefully research particular institutions, providers and websites, and read reviews and articles about them, before you commit to any. It is a matter of common sense that household names, or institutions which have existed for very many years, will tend to be safer bets than companies that you have not heard of, or which are new. If you are in doubt about these kinds of areas, speak to others or take professional advice before you commit to financial products.

Resources

Where I give examples about rates of tax and National Insurance in this book, I use English rates. Note that Scottish, Welsh and (sometimes) Northern Irish rates may be different.

I quote rates that are correct at the time of publication, but tax rates and thresholds often change, so the information in this book should be used as a guide, not a precise tool for calculation. You can always find up-to-date information on rates on HMRC's website, at: www.gov.uk/income-tax-rates.

Exceptional events can cause unexpected changes to financial rules; the schemes used during the pandemic between 2020 and 2022 were an obvious example. I don't deal with such changes in this book, but do make sure you are plugged into sources of information that can help you as and when they happen; for example, Equity www.equity.org.uk, *The Stage* www.thestage.co.uk, or our company's blog at www.accounting4actors.co.uk/news.

Keeping up to date

The vast majority of information in this book is likely to continue to be true exactly as I've described it for many years to come. However, the government sets out (at least one) Budget every year, in which all sorts of rules around taxation, benefits, pensions, etc. can change, as can rates, percentages and thresholds; and this book is being published in the early stages of roll-out for a whole new system for filing taxes – 'Making Tax Digital' (we'll get into this in detail in Chapter 2, don't worry). If, therefore, you are reading this book in 2027, or after, it is worth checking for updates to *any paragraph marked with a vertical grey line, like this one*. Where a figure might change, such as the specific amount for a tax rate or a threshold, it is only marked the first time it appears.

You will find these updates, carefully researched and written by me, and page-referenced to the relevant paragraph, on this book's dedicated updates webpage: www.nickhernbooks.co.uk/money-resources.

If there's no update listed there, then the paragraph you're reading in the book is still true.

Sources of help and advice

If you are an actor, then Equity's tax and welfare information system and helpdesk are brilliant resources, well worth the modest annual cost of Equity membership, even before you consider all the many other benefits of being a member.

The other entertainment unions, e.g. BECTU and the MU, similarly offer helpful and effective advice services.

HMRC's online resources at www.hmrc.gov.uk may help you with some basics, but I do not boast idly when I say that this book offers you better advice on detailed points than they do. (Some of the reasons for this are discussed in Chapter 2.)

Our blog archive at www.accounting4actors.co.uk/news has years'-worth of articles that discuss many of the matters raised in this book, some in much more detail.

There are also very helpful pages available from the Low Income Tax Reform Group at www.litrg.org.uk.

Martin Lewis's website (www.moneysavingexpert.com) does not have any specific advice for creative industry people as such, but it remains a good all-round source of general advice on very many basic matters from mortgages to pensions to insurance.

Disability Arts Online (www.disabilityarts.online) offers, among other things, lots of useful and detailed advice to assist disabled artists.

If you have a particular detailed question, then it can sometimes be a good idea to post it on one of the Facebook groups that cater for UK actors and/or creatives. You need to consider judiciously the quality of any advice you receive in that way – anybody could reply without any idea of what they are talking about – but these groups are often frequented by several of the specialist accountants and advisers who work in these fields, and if you are lucky, you may well get a free and high-quality answer.

Introducing Alex Actor

Alex Actor, who graduated from the acting course at the Springfield Academy of Drama in July 2025, has very generously agreed to assist us free of charge in this book by being our 'model' for various situations. We hope you enjoy Alex's company as much as we do. They are a wonderful actor and all-round amazing human being. After graduation, Alex moved into a shared flat in Hoxton with three friends from Springfield and embarked on swathes of auditions and self-tapes. In their spare time, Alex enjoys reading, travel, hiking, doing Kenneth Williams impressions, going to the gym, and slap-up Sunday pub lunches. Alex would like to take this opportunity to thank their parents for everything they have done for Alex over the years.

And the first thing that Alex must do as they settle into the Hoxton flat, after putting up their Arctic Monkeys poster, of course? They must settle down with a pencil, a notepad, and a blank Excel spreadsheet: ready to write a budget.

1. Budgeting

The very first thing to think about when you begin to consider your financial position in relation to your creative activities is budgeting. Put simply, Alex should set out with a detailed plan to earn significantly more money than they spend.

Why? Well, nothing has changed since Dickens' Mr Micawber told us: '*Annual income twenty pounds, annual expenditure nineteen six, result happiness; Annual income twenty pounds, annual expenditure twenty pounds nought and six, result misery.*' He was right in 1850 and he'd still be right now. This is the *sine qua non* of any financial plan, personal or business, long-term or short-term.

Alex must learn not to be apprehensive about the concept of making a detailed financial plan, and must arm themselves with the very few basic tools needed to get over this low hurdle. It may be tempting to Alex to ignore the issue, to think that it will take care of itself. Or perhaps Alex could appeal to the Universe to exempt them from the obligation to budget because 'I'm really not good at that kind of thing' and 'I'm so busy trying to get work'.

But if Alex does this, they make a basic mistake that it will be hard to overcome. They have in fact already achieved very many things in their life that are way harder, and take way longer to achieve, than the compilation of a basic budget. C'mon Alex – let's do this.

A budget is simply, in this context, a list of predicted income and expenses that will occur over a specified period of time. I suggest that Alex is best off thinking of a *monthly* budget. They can then easily convert any line of their budget, if they need to:

- To an *annual* budget by multiplying x 12; for example, because they need to predict how much to set aside for tax; and then…

- To a *weekly* budget by dividing ÷ 52; for example, because it is easier to think of an allowance for food or entertainment on a weekly basis.

In order to budget, Alex must list all the expenses they predict. The result may look like this:

Item	£ per month
Rent	1,000
Bills	100
Food	400
Clothes	150
Entertainment/social	350
Phone	25
Haircuts	30
Travel	100
Beauty/make-up	25
Other – e.g. Spotlight, stationery	20

So Alex is going to spend at least £2,200 per month or £26,400 per year. Let's round that up to £30,000, because it is a common mistake in the modern human mind to underestimate expenses, and because we are much better off overestimating expenses than underestimating them.

If Alex looks at their outturn at the end of the period (the 'budget' says what we *think* will happen, and the 'outturn' says what *did* happen) they will be much happier if they have underspent on expenses than if they have overspent.

A word about apps and software that can assist you in this process: if you have access to Excel or its Google Sheets equivalent, then you may already know how to construct lists and simple formulae. If you don't know, an hour or so with any of the thousands of YouTube tutorials on this will be an hour well spent.

Banking apps like Monzo, Tide, Starling and others all allow you to easily categorise expenditure as you go along, usually without any charge. You can quite easily set up your monthly budget in Excel, then download your actual bank transactions as a .csv file from your bank, cut and paste them into your sheet, and see at a glance how you performed in a particular month against your original budget.

(Later we will discuss more complex apps such as QuickBooks and Xero which can be used to prepare and submit your tax returns as well as doing more complex kinds of reporting on your income and expenditure, although these usually cost a bit more per month than the banking apps which are often free, or included with charges that you are going to pay anyway.)

Having tackled the expenditure side of the budget, Alex should now consider predicted income. This can be a harder exercise, with many more variables and fewer certainties. But we should recognise that it is unlikely that Alex will earn £30,000 from creative work in their first or indeed their second year. Some reasonably common exceptions to this rule would be if Alex lands a year-long contract in a West End or touring musical, or gets a big TV role. And if Alex were in another creative discipline, such as stage management, for example, they would be more likely to reach that target from creative engagements. But Equity say that two-thirds of their members earn less than £10,000 per year from acting.

Alex must not simply follow Mr Micawber's other famous piece of advice – that 'something will turn up'. It might do, in the event; and Alex will certainly find that they need to spend a lot of time and mental energy in protecting their belief that the strength of their intention to succeed in the creative industries will lead to, or help lead to, a positive outcome. But at the same time, Alex cannot just passively hope that the phone will ring at just the right moment to help pay the rent. They need a workable plan that will deliver say £20,000 of ordinary income per year, around £1,500 per month or £400 per week, which will support their acting business in its first two years at least.

Pause for a second if, here, you are tempted to cry, '*But that's impossible! Unfair! How can anyone do that? And I've spent years (and a lot of money) training so that I can earn my living in the way I chose! Why should I do something else?*' In fact, I do not think this position is unfair or unreasonable. It's simply a reflection of the fact that when you are setting out in the creative industries, you are *an entrepreneur with a startup*, just like any other entrepreneur with a startup in any other field.

Just as the young Alan Sugar thought to himself, 'I could flog these cheap computers'; just as somewhere, in some room right now, a budding Bill Gates is thinking, 'I've invented the app that everyone will use in five years' time'; so Alex is thinking in entirely the same way, in business terms, when they think, 'What the London stage and Netflix need right now is *me*.'

And just as Alan Sugar and Bill Gates started by capitalising their businesses – raising money to pay for what they needed to get started, and paying that back over time in any of several ways – so Alex needs to capitalise their acting business. The most common way to do this is, in effect, to subsidise acting earnings with other kinds of earnings.

The best ways of doing this are, of course, up to the individual, but some of the most obvious and everyday ways we see of achieving it are:

- 'A job in a pub' – any relatively low-paid and low-skilled work that can be done in say thirty hours per week, especially if some of these hours can be done in the evenings, leaving you with say twenty to thirty hours of available daytimes.

- 'A flexible day-job' – many creative individuals use their skills in other areas to keep part-time jobs in other fields. These are many and varied, and obviously this works best the more flexible the other job is. (Hint: there are even actors working part-time for our accountancy company, working from home and choosing whatever hours are convenient to them. A tax return compiled at one o'clock in the morning looks the same as one compiled at four in the afternoon.)

- 'Related fields' – many earn money from teaching creative skills to adults or children, being a personal trainer or teaching yoga, or through contracts with the many business training firms that use creative methods of corporate coaching.

- **Self-producing** – we will discuss this in more detail in Chapter 7. There are many ways of doing something entrepreneurial with your skillset that generate income while also allowing you to develop producing skills, from touring your own show, to organising children's parties, to starting a stand-up night in your local pub.

So it's up to Alex (and to you). There are as many different ways of solving this conundrum as there are creative industry workers in the UK – but almost everyone is solving it somehow.

Now Alex just needs to set aside half an hour at the end of every month to track their budget as time goes on, to see if their predictions are correct. And if the plan is not working, Alex must change it – not just carry on with Micawber-like faith. It really is as simple as that.

So, the next step: armed with a basic income strategy, a budget, a list of helpful resources and, of course, with this book on the desk, doubling handily as a coaster for their morning coffee – let Alex set sail into the world of tax.

Golden rules for budgeting

- Don't find an excuse not to do it.
- Overestimate your expenses and underestimate your income, not the other way round.
- Review your budget regularly.

2. Tax Basics and Getting Started

In this chapter I'm going to take Alex on a journey around their first tax return. Alex has many questions about this process, and I'll try to answer as many as I can.

We'll cover some key definitions and deadlines, consider why the system works as it does, and think about some basics such as record-keeping and all the things Alex needs to get done not just to comply, but to make the financial system work for them as best they can.

Before we get started, it is worth getting five key definitions straight in our heads – these will come up all the time and they need to be terms we all understand instinctively.

PAYE – this stands for Pay As You Earn, and is the tax system for most workers in the UK, because they are in employment. They work for (usually) one person or one company, often long-term.

Self-assessment – this is the tax system for people who pay tax in other ways, whether that be instead of or as well as PAYE.

Self-employment – this is the main reason why somebody pays tax through self-assessment and not PAYE; because they work for themselves. Lots of different people pay them to do stuff over the year, not just one company. The overwhelming majority of creatives are in this category.

Freelance – this is simply a synonym for self-employment.

Sole trader – this is the technical tax description of a person who is self-employed under their own steam and is not working in a Partnership or a Limited Company (much more on these in Chapters 6 and 7).

What is a tax return?

A tax return is a long, boring, overcomplicated form which approximately one-third of the UK's adult population is legally obliged to use, to report their financial affairs to HMRC (His Majesty's Revenue and Customs) and to calculate how much tax they owe for the year in question. The other two-thirds don't need to, either because they pay all their tax PAYE, or because they don't reach a certain threshold of earned income.

Every adult in the UK can open an online account with the State which is called a Government Gateway. At the time of writing, the self-assessment tax return can be submitted online through your Government Gateway, although this will change during the coming transition to Making Tax Digital – more on this later (from page 32). Alternatively, Alex's return can be submitted on their behalf by a registered accountant using their own software, or exceptionally by post (although there is an earlier deadline for this).

The UK tax year runs from 6 April to 5 April in each year, and let's not even get started on the reasons for this almost uniquely British piece of utter, stupendous nonsense which serves no purpose whatsoever other than to confuse everybody. The day after I become Emperor, we will change to 1 January to 31 December like almost everyone else in the world.

In an even less comprehensible piece of nonsense, HMRC allow Alex to simply ignore the official tax year dates *so far as self-employment goes*. Alex can choose to measure their income and expenditure – this is also called 'making up accounts' – to 31 March. So, I almost always recommend that a creative freelancer should treat their accounts year as 1 April to 31 March, which is much less confusing.

Unfortunately, other kinds of income that may be reported on the tax return (more on this later) like rental or dividend income, are always measured from 6 April to 5 April. The count of days in the year that may be needed to determine tax residency (also more coming on this later) also works between the official dates. So, Alex can only use 1 April to 31 March to measure freelance work earnings, if they choose to, and not to measure other matters relevant to the tax year.

After the tax year ends on 5 April, the deadline for HMRC to receive a completed online self-assessment return for that year is 31 January, about ten months later. So Alex's deadline for their 2025/26 return is 31 January 2027. This is also the deadline to pay any tax which is owed in respect of the 2025/26 year.

This is a third, almost uniquely British, piece of nonsense – Alex is not required to report what happened in their business on 6 April 2025 until 31 January 2027, nearly two years later! If Alex happened to shoot a huge ad on 6 April 2025, they still won't pay the tax on that fee until two years after it. That fact places an immediate burden on Alex to have excellent, long-lasting record-keeping, and also to make careful savings as regards tax payments.

Alex *could* file their 2025/26 return any day between 6 April 2026 and 31 January 2027, if they had all the necessary information as early as 6 April, including things like interest statements from their bank, and a P60 from any PAYE jobs. Approximately 10% of all tax returns are filed on 31 January itself, or indeed late. I warmly recommend that Alex tries to get themselves into the 90%, because things get very stressful for the 10%.

Alex will be penalised by HMRC if they do not meet the 31 January deadline. The penalty will be at least £100, rising to £300 after three months, plus interest and further penalties added to any amounts of tax which were due and which are paid late. So it is important to get ahead of the game and plan to get everything filed and paid on time, otherwise Alex will just be wasting money on unnecessary fines.

HMRC accept a very limited range of excuses for late filing, such as having a serious illness or dealing with the death of a close relative. They do not accept excuses such as – and here are some real examples of excuses that have formed the basis of unsuccessful appeals – the dog eating all your receipts, your mother-in-law being a witch who put a curse on you, or the death of your goldfish.

Who checks my return?

Different tax authorities round the world have different systems, and different extents to which they police self-assessment in its various forms. The UK has a notably light touch in this respect, compared to other regimes. It is very likely that no human will ever check the information that you present in a particular year. This is not an excuse for you to cheat, or to present information for which you have no evidence, for two reasons: first, to do so is manifestly unfair to all your friends, neighbours and colleagues; and second, in the albeit unlikely event that your return *is* inspected and checked, you will be in very big trouble if you are found to have given false information.

Why are so many rules about tax 'grey areas'?

We are used to a world in which compliance with law tends to be a very clear matter. Where the speed limit is 30 miles per hour, we understand that it is a crime to drive at 31mph, even though we realise that the police and the magistrate will be likely to be more lenient with us for driving at 31mph than at 50mph.

We are also used to a society in which most people know enough about most of the rules that matter to go about their daily life. Most drivers know all the important rules of driving, and have passed a test on these; most people who play cricket know most of or all the rules of cricket.

Tax is not like this. In the first place, it's a vast topic. There are over a hundred different taxes in the UK. The Finance Act 2024, which runs to more than six hundred pages, is only one of about ten Acts that govern tax rules, all of which have hundreds of chapters, with a new Finance Act adjusted most years. There is no one person, or even small group of people, who have expert knowledge of all of this. When you become a solicitor, you don't get tested on the *whole* law, and similarly, when you become an accountant or a tax inspector, you don't get tested on *everything* about tax – it would be impossible.

A further 'challenge to knowledge' presented by tax is that tax laws might apply to people differently in different situations. You break the traffic law by driving through a red traffic light regardless of whether you are driving a green car, a black taxi or a blue van. But there are different tax laws for companies vs. individuals; for farmers vs. doctors; for people earning £X vs. people earning £Y. I gave just three examples in that sentence, and you see already that nine different situations apply. Think about a Limited Company running a farm and earning £100,000 as opposed to a sole trader plumber earning £20,000. Now imagine those three variations, with their matrix of nine different situations, multiplied by all the variables that occur in the world of business income.

In fact, with such variety afforded by the real world, it is rather surprising that anything very definite about tax can be stated at all. And one of the main reasons it can is because of the mechanism of tribunals and legal precedent.

All the time, taxpayers and their advisors are considering how law X or law Y should be applied in their situation. Every day, situations arise in relation to someone's tax position that have never arisen in quite the same way before. And it happens sometimes that a taxpayer will make a return which HMRC says has been drawn up too leniently, or conversely that HMRC will make a demand on a taxpayer that the taxpayer says is too harsh.

If the matter is arguable – and it often is – and if neither side will back down, it gets resolved by a tax tribunal, which is simply the equivalent of the court system in the world of tax. At a tax tribunal, either a single judge or two judges (depending on the level of the case) will hear both the taxpayer and HMRC put their case, and will issue a judgement, which is then binding in that case, and which also then helps provide a precedent when a similar situation arises again. The tribunal judges are usually either very senior and experienced accountants and/or tax lawyers. (In the unlikely event that you are interested in what sorts of matters generally get taken to tribunal, feel free to look up some cases here: www.gov.uk/tax-tribunal-decisions. If you are still awake after ten minutes of reading, consider whether you should give up your career as an actor-screenwriter and become a tax lawyer instead.)

And a particular problem for creative industry taxpayers is that very, very few relevant tribunal cases have ever been brought in our sector. An exception is some well-known recent cases where star names and HMRC have fought specifically over an area known as 'IR35': a narrow question limited to employment status, which we will discuss later very briefly, but which is probably of no more than passing interest to you. We will discuss the notable relevant tribunal cases later in this book (in Chapter 4), but as you will see, there have been only half a dozen in total, in the hundred-plus-year history of the present income tax system.

This reflects two simple facts. First, creative industry businesses are a niche – they tend to be small relative to other industries and disciplines. Second, they tend in most cases to generate less money than other industries. And so, quite logically, the tax tribunals' time tends to be taken up with cases that apply to larger businesses, more taxpayers and that involve conflicts over larger sums of money.

It may well be logical; but it leaves us with a challenge. It means that many questions which apply to the everyday matter of taxing a sole tradership in the creative industries have never been tested at tribunal.

For example, I would usually advise a stage manager that a subscription to *The Stage* newspaper is an allowable business expense for their particular trade. But that has never been tested at tribunal. HMRC have never challenged that point. So nobody can be absolutely sure; and this accounts for the reason why it may be very hard for you, from time to time, to get an entirely straight answer to your questions about tax. There is, fortunately or unfortunately, no single source of information to which you can turn to resolve every question beyond doubt. The best course of action is to use this book and the resources we recommend.

Taxpayers sometimes make the intuitive but unfortunately wrong assumption that because HMRC have *processed* a return, they have *agreed* it. Not so. HMRC's policy on analysing self-assessment returns is called, internally, 'Process Then Check'. I suggest that a more accurate name would be 'We Will Process Whatever Old Rubbish Anyone Feels Like Sending Us And Then We May Or May Not Decide Up To Six Years Later That Actually We Didn't Like It'. You cannot assume that just because they have processed something you have done for years and years, it is correct.

Are HMRC themselves a helpful resource for tax advice?

I mean, you kind of think they should be, right? We are used to a world in which the professional side of a relationship takes responsibility for, and does its best to assist, the consumer side. And HMRC even call you their 'customer'. So they should be ready and able to answer your questions – right? On their *helpline*…it should give *help*… right?

Well – up to a point… but I'm afraid it's quite a limited point.

First, it is comparatively hard even to reach HMRC by phone, if you have a question that you want to put in simple terms to a human respondent. In 2024, HMRC's average wait time for callers was twenty-three minutes – more than four times longer than the average wait time to get through to your bank. Some calls, say at 3 p.m. on Christmas Eve, are answered much more quickly than that, so it follows that at busy weekday times some folks are waiting an hour or more (and then, of course, you lose signal, get cut off and go back to the back of the queue...).

Second, consider that there are around 50,000 people working for HMRC and that the vast majority of them don't have anything to do with self-employment of any kind, let alone in a specialist niche like the creative industries. Most of those 50,000 are dealing with the big numbers: Payroll, employment benefits, National Insurance, Corporation Tax, VAT, Business Rates, Capital Gains, Land and Property, not to mention the raft of internal organisation and back-office functions... you and Alex just aren't on the radar of 95+% of tax inspectors.

So let's say there might be a couple of thousand staff at HMRC who properly understand self-employment. Now consider again my remarks in the section above, about how specialised niche, small industries are, in relation to tax law. Almost none of these couple of thousand HMRC staff know anything at all about any small, specialised industries.

So if you make a random call on a random day answered by a random person, and ask if an actor can deduct the cost of their haircuts, you are probably asking someone who has never considered that question before, doesn't know what a headshot or a showreel is, and doesn't know anything about the process of casting, agents, self-tapes, casting directors, etc... all of which you would need to understand to be able to answer that question reliably. I am confident that if you called HMRC five times to ask that question, you would not receive exactly the same answer twice. (By the way the correct answer, as we will discuss in more detail in Chapter 4, is 'Probably'.) Our tax system, hard though this is to appreciate, relies on the support of private advisers.

HMRC are good at, and are worth consulting on, *process* questions, such as when your return is due, and any technical issues you are having logging into your account and seeing what you should be able to see there, etc.

Beyond those types of narrow matters, if you want to seek HMRC's opinion, follow the same advice given by *The Hitchhiker's Guide to the Galaxy* to those thinking of hitching a ride on a Vogon spaceship: Forget it. Use this book and the other resources it points you towards.

Does that mean I need an accountant?

Disclaimer – this book is not a commercial. I have not charged you the price of this book so that I can tell you that in fact you need to spend twenty times more to engage me, or one of my professional colleagues. Promise.

But if you *don't* need us, then how is it that I have a viable business? There are two general answers: one to do with self-assessment and the other to do with Limited Companies.

Around 60% of self-assessment returns are completed without the assistance of accountants and tax advisors, and I believe that a similar proportion can and indeed should apply to creative industry taxpayers: about two-thirds of you should be able to deal with this yourselves, using this book and the other resources we recommend. Having said that, we'll discuss Making Tax Digital later on in this chapter. It is early days for this new system, but some accountants believe it may well reduce that 60%, because it will make it a bit harder to file on your own.

The other 40% probably fall into one or more of these categories:

i. People earning more than £50,000 per year, and/or those who are VAT-registered. We will discuss VAT registration in more detail later, but we would always recommend professional assistance for those in this category simply because the numbers are bigger and the stakes are higher. Up to £50K, a UK taxpayer pays 20% tax; beyond that, 40% tax (at least). So you are doubling the effect of some mistakes if mistakes are made. And the VAT system is much more complex and frightening than the income tax system.

ii. Those who have worked overseas in the year, or who are required to file a tax return in another country as well as in the UK. I'll briefly touch on this huge topic later in this chapter, but it is so complex that I can't provide the necessary answers to all questions here. If you are in this position, most accountants agree it is just best for you to accept that it is too complex and too full of potential pitfalls to handle by yourself. I see more mistakes made on this by clients who come to me after trying to do it themselves – or trying to do their UK return assisted by an accountant overseas – than I do in any other area.

iii. People who don't like doing their return themselves, or are anxious about writing the wrong thing and getting into trouble. There is no shame in being anxious about this. Many people would prefer to pay a modest fee to be spared anxiety.

iv. If you want to get a mortgage and the prospective mortgager insists that your accounts are signed by an accountant. Sometimes they do, sometimes they don't.

Only you can decide if you want professional help or not; it's a bit like DIY vs. GSI in plumbing or painting: you can probably do it yourself, but the job should be better and last longer if done by a qualified pro.

If you do decide to use an accountant, then as discussed in the Introduction (okay, it's a fair cop, this sentence *is* the commercial break) you should use one of the handful of specialist firms that practise heavily in the creative industries in Great Britain (okay, okay, like mine, I said it). Remember, as I said, that tax is big, and contains hundreds of different specialisms. Accountants who don't specialise in creatives just don't know what your working day is like. If you choose one, you will just spend time and energy that you don't need to spend in educating them about it.

We'll discuss Limited Companies in more detail later. If you decide you want to form your own, then you absolutely need an accountant – you will not be able to report taxes for a Limited Company correctly yourself.

What is Making Tax Digital?

The mid to late 2020s bring a huge change in the way that self-assessment works technically. This gives Alex three immediate additional headaches:

i. Not only do they have to understand the basics of self-assessment, they are also getting started at a time at which the system is changing.

ii. In previous years they could have benefitted from 'Green Room' advice from older, more experienced folks, much of which will not now apply because even the more experienced folks are going to need to get to grips with the new system.

iii. At the time of writing this book, some of the details of Making Tax Digital are still undecided, so Alex will need to look at some of the online resources we reference to get themselves up to date about some of the things I have written here.

Since around 2015, HMRC has been developing this very significant overhaul of the self-assessment system. Its goal is to collect all returns from self-employed taxpayers on a basis that differs from the old system in two ways:

i. With a quarterly, not annual, report (though *payments* will still be annual).

ii. With a report sent to them through bespoke software, and not using the present system of typing numbers into the form on their website.

At the time of writing, the timetable for the introduction of Making Tax Digital for Income Tax and Self-Assessment (MTDITSA) is:

Summer 2022	MTD live and compulsory for VAT returns.
April 2026	MTDITSA live for those with income over £50,000 in the previous year. Note two very important things here: First, the MTD threshold is a threshold of *income* at £50,000, not *profits* at £50,000; whereas the threshold for paying 40% tax is the other way round. Second, only income from self-employment and rental income is included in the MTD £50,000 threshold – not PAYE, dividend income, capital gains, or anything else.

| April 2027 | MTDITSA live for those earning income of £30,000+. |
| April 2028 | MTDITSA live for most or all self-employed taxpayers. |

The timetable has changed several times and is still, in 2025, subject to change. But as you can see, it is quite likely that as you are reading this book, these changes may already apply to you.

If this is all news to you, therefore, and you have been used in the past to submitting an annual return by typing out your numbers on the HMRC website, you will need quite urgently to reconsider what to do, and take further advice from the sources of information listed from page 11.

Many experienced taxpayers are frustrated with HMRC and the government for introducing this change (by the way, a Conservative government started it, a Labour government progressed it). Many feel that the system was working fine before and that the new requirements are an additional and unwelcome burden and bureaucracy. But defenders of MTD say that the old system is out-of-date and too imprecise, and allows too much scope for cash-based businesses such as taxi firms, hairdressers and gardeners (sorry taxi firms, hairdressers and gardeners, don't take my remarks personally, I love you all) to hide undeclared income.

A further complication for creatives is that, as many with experience will know, you do not necessarily (or even ever) stay within just one of these thresholds from year to year. You might hop from £20,000 to £50,000 to £30,000 and then back again. At the time of writing, HMRC have said that once you are in Making Tax Digital, you will stay in until your turnover dips below £20,000 for three years running, but this may change in future.

Record-keeping

MTDITSA fundamentally alters the way you keep the financial records of your business, and how you report on these to HMRC.

Up till now, you will probably have been keeping your records in one of these four typical ways:

i. You already use an app such as Xero, QuickBooks, FreeAgent, SansDrama, or one of the many other options.

ii. You record all your income and expenses on a spreadsheet, dividing your expenses into obvious categories such as travel, professional appearance, etc.

iii. You don't do i) or ii) as you go along, but you are fairly organised about your bank card usage and so at the end of the year you do a big exercise adding it all up, complete with a pot of coffee and several Mars bars – and then you type all the total numbers into HMRC's website.

iv. You don't do i), ii) or even iii). You don't even think about this until the end of the year (or late January the following year), at which point you pause and consider the mountain of difficulty you have created for yourself by not doing i), ii) or iii), and you then muddle through somehow with luck and a following wind.

MTDITSA changes all this, because iii) and iv) will not be options any more, and even ii) will be tricky, because you will no longer be able to simply type your numbers out on HMRC's website. If you want to continue doing ii), you will probably need to use a spreadsheet template that you buy or beg from somewhere, and use an as-yet-unknown bit of commercial software to upload it to HMRC, or work with an accountant who will take care of this for you.

There is still a long period of change to navigate; but HMRC's ultimate goal is to push everyone towards method i), and you may be saving yourself time and trouble in the long run if you simply adopt that method now.

It's impossible for me to recommend any one record-keeping solution over another. This really is horses for courses. If you want very comprehensive records, if you find it easy to use slick IT, and if you don't mind paying a little extra, then you will probably benefit most from Xero or QuickBooks. If you would rather keep going on an Excel spreadsheet, you may struggle to find MTD-compliant cheap or free packages to help you – you may need to look at asking an accountant to help you.

Keeping receipts

However you keep your records, you are obliged to keep receipts for amounts you have spent for six years after the tax year in which you reported them.

Therefore if Alex buys a packet of pencils on 1 May 2026, they must keep the receipt until 5 April 2033. It does not matter whether they keep the receipt on paper or electronically, either as a picture in a folder on a drive, or attached to the record of a transaction in an app or cloud book-keeping system – Alex is free to choose whatever method suits them best, as long as they choose one of those methods.

I am often asked if it is okay to claim an expense for which you do not have a receipt. The answer is not straightforward. There have been inspections and tribunal cases in which evidence of expenditure which is *not* receipts has been accepted; for example, entries on bank statements, or emails from suppliers confirming that such-and-such an expense was incurred. So I tend to advise that there are everyday situations in which you should go ahead and record an expense even though you missed the receipt, especially if you don't make a habit of it.

But by not getting a receipt, you open the door for HMRC to dig their heels in and argue that the expense should not be allowed, and there have been occasions where tribunals have agreed with them. You also create a situation where time and energy is used up arguing about expenses for which, if there was a receipt, there could be no argument. So, keep receipts if you possibly can. (There is a different answer to this question if you are VAT-registered, coming in Chapter 6.)

A self-employed person is not *obliged* to use a separate bank account for business transactions (unless they are VAT-registered); but in practice, you make your life much easier if you do. So I would advise Alex to open a separate new business bank account. This is often much easier and cheaper (or free) with the so-called 'challenger' online banks such as Revolut, Monzo or Tide, rather than with the traditional high-street banks.

Alex's registration and return timeline

We learned earlier that Alex graduated from drama school in July 2025. They took a short break in Ibiza and then moved into their new shared flat in Hoxton in August

2025 and began looking for acting work, submitting self-tapes, etc.

Alex has until the end of September 2026 to register with HMRC as self-employed, from the moment when they first earn more than £3,000 in income from creative work (it may be in their interest to do this when they earn over £1,000 – we'll come back to this on page 50). They do this using a simple online form called an SA1, available on HMRC's website. After they submit this form, HMRC will write to their home address telling them their Unique Tax Reference (UTR) – a ten-digit number.

This is different to Alex's National Insurance (NI) number (two letters, six numbers, one letter) which they should have been sent automatically on their sixteenth birthday (or been given as part of the visa process if arriving in the UK as an adult). If Alex does not have their NI number for any reason then they urgently need to contact the Department for Work and Pensions helpline to get it – they will not be able to do any work of any kind without it.

While completing the SA1 form, Alex will also sign up for a Government Gateway account if they have not previously done so – the Government Gateway login is a twelve-digit number with a password chosen by the applicant. This login and password will last Alex for life and will be the way they sign into HMRC's (and some other State) services.

Alex's Government Gateway tax account has two sections:

i. A Personal Tax Account section covering PAYE, National Insurance, State Pension and any benefits.

ii. A Business Tax Account, covering self-employment and self-assessment.

Further sections can be added as necessary in future; for example, if Alex becomes VAT-registered (more on this later).

Here's a timetable of Alex's entry to the self-assessment system:

April-July 2025	Alex was completing their studies, and perhaps doing a bit of casual PAYE work on the side.
July 2025	Alex graduated.
August 2025	They started self-employed work, they continued casual PAYE work, they passed the £3,000 income threshold and they registered with HMRC as self-employed. They also started careful record-keeping, as we discussed earlier. Alex paid particular attention to this, which was very sensible.
5 April 2026	End of Alex's first tax year.
April 2026–31 January 2027	Within this period, Alex must complete and submit a tax return for 2025/26.
31 January 2027	Deadline to pay 2025/26 tax, and first payment on account (discussed later, in Chapter 3) for 2026/27. NB. Even if Alex submitted the 2025/26 return on 6 April 2026, they are still not obliged to pay any bill until 31 January 2027.

31 July 2027	Deadline to pay second payment on account for 2026/27.
	This is also the Making Tax Digital deadline for Alex's first new *quarterly* return, if they have been told to join MTD. (NB. This could still be delayed, so check information sources for updates.)
	(If Alex had already been in the system rather than a new starter, and if they had earned more than £50,000 profit in 2024/25, then this requirement would have kicked in on 31 July 2026.)

In the next chapter, we'll discuss how Alex accounts for their income, and continue their journey through the process of their first tax return and tax payments.

Golden rules for getting started

- Consider registering for self-assessment as soon as you go over £1,000 of freelance income.

- Decide on your record-keeping system and stick to it.

- Find out when you will be brought into the quarterly-reporting, Making Tax Digital system, and decide how you are going to navigate it.

3. Income and Preparing for Tax

In this chapter, we'll concentrate on different types of income, and complete Alex's preparations for making their first tax return.

One of the key matters that Alex needs to get their head round is the relationship between self-employment and PAYE income.

Self-employment vs. PAYE

Most workers in the UK in offices, shops, factories, places of education and healthcare, etc. are employed on a PAYE (Pay As You Earn) basis, and therefore do not have to submit a tax return – their tax and National Insurance is collected automatically through their salary.

Most *creative* work, however, is done through the self-employment system, rather like occupations such as taxi-driving, painting and decorating, and plumbing.

It is up to an engager, rather than you the worker, to decide whether the work they are offering you is self-employment (often called 'freelance' work) or PAYE employment. In most cases, you don't have any choice about this: engagers offer what they offer. And it doesn't really matter to you, because you pay almost exactly the same amount of tax in most cases, regardless of the method of collection.

The system was not always as comfortable on this point as it is now, and indeed some arguments about employment vs. self-employment do still rage in the courts – there have been high-profile cases on this issue for entertainers and presenters like Lorraine Kelly and Adrian Chiles.

In the 1990s, Equity fought a protracted battle to shore up self-employment status for actors, stage managers and TV/film technicians, which was largely successful. They have also succeeded in the more recent past in securing many of the benefits of employment – such as mandatory pension contribution – even in self-employment contracts for creatives, which is a great win for all involved.

In practice, therefore, the great majority of contracts that Alex will be offered today will be self-employment contracts. But even if they are PAYE, this should not present them with a big problem (though note comments that follow in Chapter 4 about PAYE employees claiming deductible expenses).

'Day-jobs' and their relationship to your creative self-employment – P45s, P60s, etc.

Many – in fact in my experience *most* – creative workers accept jobs in other fields during the year, whether part-time, full-time, short-term, regular, etc. These jobs can be anything from teaching to admin work, to sales work, to landscape gardening. In our firm we call these 'day-jobs' despite the conscious misnomer – they might easily be done at night, after all.

'Day-jobs' are more likely, but not exclusively so, to be PAYE jobs rather than freelance jobs, because it is more likely that in doing them you are *assisting someone else with their business rather than conducting your own business*. Think about how this principle clearly applies, for example, to taking shifts in a bar or a shop.

Bear in mind, though, that you might view as *your* day-job at least two other kinds of activities which are usually not PAYE, but additional freelancing:

- Doing something related to your creative discipline but not the same as your main creative discipline; for example, if you are an actor, privately tutoring A-level Drama students.

- Doing something entirely different to your creative discipline but doing it under your own steam, finding your clients yourself and contracting directly with them and not through an employer. For example, many creatives in the UK who speak a language other than English, take on translating or language-teaching work.

Unless someone has given you an employment contract and is giving you payslips and a P60 at the end of the year, these kinds of work (even though you think of them as day-jobs) are not PAYE: they are simply additional freelancing.

When you fill in your annual tax return, you should treat all creative work as belonging to one self-employment business – what HMRC calls a trade. You should do this even if the types of work are not, to your expert eye, the same type of work. But for HMRC's purposes, there is no need to distinguish between acting and voice-coaching, or between directing and designing sets, or between producing and tutoring A-level Drama students.

(An exception to this is if you are being paid healthy amounts to create things on commission, such as writing books or articles, or making sculptures or visual art. This creates a unique, highly technical reason to choose to separate that work from other types of creative work, because it may help you to stay in a lower tax band if you report this income separately. If this is you, seek specialist advice – the nuances here are too complex for you to deal with DIY.)

If, by contrast, your other freelancing has nothing to do with creative work – you are walking dogs, selling calculators, or trading in widgets – then you should treat this activity as a second trade in your tax return and in your quarterly updates for MTD. You will complete two sets of self-employment pages in your tax return, although it will still only be one return and you still have only one UTR.

Alex, listening carefully to our advice about budgeting and capitalising their new business in Chapter 1, has decided to sign up for casual 'zero-hours' work at an independent clothing store in Shoreditch which is owned and managed by a friend of theirs, Lauren.

As we noted above, it is Lauren's responsibility, not Alex's, to determine whether she offers this work to Alex PAYE or freelance. She will in all probability conclude or be advised by her accountant that she should offer it PAYE, because she sets all the parameters for the work – she decides on the time and place of the work and the way that the work is done.

This means that Alex will not have to invoice (another word for 'bill') Lauren, but rather that Lauren will put Alex on the shop's payroll system, and give them a payslip every week or month, automatically deducting any tax or National Insurance that Alex owes.

HMRC will send Lauren a tax code for Alex when she tells them that she has started Alex on the shop payroll. The tax code is an attempt by HMRC to get the correct amount of tax collected, based on their understanding of Alex's overall earnings.

On 5 April in any year, Alex will either still be working for Lauren or will have left. They need either one of two forms, a P60 or a P45, to show how much Lauren paid them during the year.

- If they are still working there, Lauren will issue a P60.
- If Alex has left, Lauren will have issued a P45 on the date they left.

Either way, if Alex worked PAYE for Lauren during the year, Lauren is legally obliged to have given Alex either a P60 or a P45 by 31 May of the new tax year.

It is remarkable how often this simple requirement is overlooked, but Alex (and you) really need to grasp it if you are going to get your tax return correct.

Some creatives think that their tax return is only for their freelancing and that they should not mention their PAYE work on it. *This is wrong.* The self-assessment tax return should always contain a report of *all* income received from all earnings, as well as a note of any PAYE tax that has been deducted (because if it has been deducted, it is not owed again). Alex's tax return will be a snapshot of *all* their income and expenses for the year.

As I mentioned earlier, all PAYE employees are given a tax code for the year. The tax code is only relevant to the year in which it is issued, and can change during the year. The tax code represents an attempt by HMRC to estimate how much tax your employer should deduct PAYE. They often estimate correctly, but sometimes not.

For most creative workers, toggling between PAYE and self-employment through the year, the tax code is not a matter of much importance, because the retrospective self-assessment return for the year will analyse the whole question of how much they made, how much tax they owe, and how much of that tax if any they have already paid PAYE and do not therefore still owe.

If you think your tax code is causing some significant error now, *within the year to which it relates*, then it is worth investigating further to ensure that you don't pay too much too early. Otherwise, in most circumstances, you do not need to worry about it, and you should wait for the annual tax return process to establish exactly what you owed and to sort out any underpayment or overpayment.

There is an issue that can cause confusion to performers and stage managers, who are often paid weekly by producers. It comes about if you are presented with a weekly payslip showing the tax code as 'NT'. This *looks* like a PAYE employment payment, but it *isn't*. It's just an advice that they have settled your agent's invoice. You know this because of the 'NT' tax code – 'NT' means, in effect, 'this isn't PAYE employment as such'.

Equity contracts oblige producers to tell you how much they are paying you every week, and so some producers are in the habit of using their automated payroll system to produce advice payslips. Unfortunately, this means that they sometimes report the pay automatically to HMRC, and unfortunately this sometimes makes HMRC pre-populate your tax return with it as employment earnings, in the same way that they might do if you had done some shifts in a pub or a shop and been paid PAYE. *But this is wrong*, because of the nature of your contract with the producer. You need to move this income from the employment section of your tax return to the self-employment section, even if HMRC have pre-populated it the other way round. Understandably this is rather confusing, but I'm afraid that's just how it is.

This issue became a real problem for some unfortunate actors and stage managers during the Covid crisis. The self-employment support grants were calculated according to average self-employment earnings – PAYE earnings were ignored. This meant that, exceptionally cruelly, people who had not spotted this problem in earlier years were denied grants which they would have received if this simple admin error had not happened to them. Our firm and Equity tried very, very hard to get HMRC to shift on this but we didn't succeed. So it is very important that you are aware of this matter, if you ever receive NT-code payslips.

National Insurance

Alex was discussing all these matters one day in the green room with Shobu, a very experienced actor, and Shobu said in passing 'and you have to pay your NI, of course'. Alex was just about to ask Shobu to explain this when the kettle boiled and the moment passed. So Alex is still wondering about it.

National Insurance (NI, or sometimes NIC, National Insurance Contributions) is effectively a euphemism for an additional form of tax. It is a sum of money that you have to pay the State so that it can spend it for public benefit. Traditionally, it is money ringfenced for spending on pensions and low-income benefits, and it has always been subject to rules slightly different to tax rules, as regards the way it is collected.

PAYE employees pay their NI by deduction (called Class 1 NICs) from their wages, in the same way that they pay income tax, subject to various thresholds.

Self-employed people, however, pay their NI as part of the tax return process. The amounts owed depend on how much you earn. You may pay Class 2 NICs, which is a comparatively modest flat fee per week of self-employment; and you may also pay Class 4 NICs, payable once your earnings are over a certain level.

(Hang on, what happened to Class 3? Oh look, there it is: Class 3 NICs is the name given to certain types of other contributions; for example, those made by UK citizens living overseas for a time.)

The amounts and thresholds for NI change regularly, so we will not quote any actual numbers here and you can always check the up-to-date ones under 'Rates and allowances: National Insurance contributions' on www.gov.uk.

When you make your correct NI contributions in a particular tax year, that year is marked on your NI record (tagged to the NI number that you were given when you first started working in the UK) as a 'Full Year'.

Once you have ten Full Years, you begin to be entitled to the State Pension when you reach retirement age; and once you have thirty-five Full Years, you are entitled to the full State Pension. Thus, for most people, the important thing about the NI system is to check that you are on track to reach thirty-five Full Years before retirement age. You may also need a certain number of Full Years on your record to qualify for certain benefits at an *earlier* time of your life; you qualify for these depending on which benefit it is, and how many Full Years you have contributed relative to how many years you have been working.

For many people earning average or high amounts, there will often not be any need to think about your NI – it will take care of itself. You will pay either PAYE or through your self-assessment tax return, and the year will be marked as 'Full' automatically. You can check your record of Full Years any time via your Government Gateway account.

An issue will arise, however, if you are earning *below* the threshold to make an automatic contribution, or if you have a break from working in the UK. This often happens when, for example, new starters are surviving on a very low income, perhaps supported by family members or living with parents; or when people live and work overseas for a time, or take a career break to care for family members.

If you do not make an automatic contribution in a given year, you can choose to make a voluntary contribution. If you have some years of low earnings, it is vital that you make sufficient voluntary contributions to ensure that you reach that thirty-five Full Year mark, and this is likely to be the best long-term investment of any kind that you can possibly ever make.

Voluntary contributions cost around £200 per year, and every additional Full Year adds about £350 to your State Pension for a year – so, assuming you enjoy a retirement of say fifteen years, you will get more than £5,000 back for your £200, and your 75-year-old self will be very grateful to your young self for having been careful about this issue.

So if you earn below the NI threshold in a year, or if you have a break from work, you should strongly consider a voluntary contribution. Contributions must be made by the payment deadline for the tax year concerned (i.e. by 31 January for the previous tax year). There is a mechanism by which voluntary contributions can be made late for years which have been missed, up to a point, but this is generally much more expensive than simply paying on time.

HMRC does not, to date, have a brilliant track record at getting all digital record-keeping accurate. One of the most frustrating manifestations of this is that when you have any kind of break from NI contributions, you can subsequently find that when you resume contributing, your contributions do not correctly land in your NI record and instead just sit as an unallocated credit in your self-assessment account, where they can be hard to spot because the system is labyrinthine. Look out for this, make a quick check once a year that your NI record is accumulating Full Years correctly, and speak to HMRC if it does not look like it's working properly.

Thresholds

Now we need to introduce the concept of the various income thresholds, and consider why they are important.

£1,000

We have already mentioned one relevant income threshold: you saw on page 38 that Alex should consider registering for self-assessment as soon as their freelance income in a tax year exceeds £1,000. Between £1,000 and £3,000 they will be asked to use a simple online platform to declare the earnings and pay any tax due, without submitting a full tax return.

£3,000

If your income exceeds £3,000, you must submit a full tax return, even if you don't owe any tax.

£6,725

However, Alex will not be obliged to pay NI until their freelance profits are over £6,725 (although as discussed above, it is a very good idea to pay NI voluntarily if their profits are lower).

£12,570

£12,570 is the threshold below which Alex does not pay income tax on their earnings. To put this another way – everyone is allowed to earn £12,570 without paying any tax on that (except that once Alex goes past £100,000 earnings in the year, this allowance will be eroded).

£30,000

Nor will they pay student loan repayments until their profits go over another threshold, which is approximately £30,000 depending on the type of loan.

The £1,000, £3,000 and £6,725 thresholds only apply to Alex's self-employment.

The £12,570 and £30,000 thresholds, however, apply to *all* of Alex's taxable profits and pay, *including* anything received from PAYE work on the side.

This last point tends to cause some confusion, though the principle is very simple. The £12,570 personal allowance is an allowance on *all income regardless of its source*. You don't get one free £12,570 chunk for self-employment *and* another one for PAYE.

Remember that it is a common mistake for those working both freelance and PAYE to think that their tax return will only cover freelance work and that PAYE work has already been reported and taken care of by the employer, and that therefore they should not write down their PAYE income on their return. This, as noted before, is *wrong*.

The self-assessment tax return is a snapshot of *all* income and expenses. Do not worry that by including PAYE work on it, you will be taxed twice on that work – you will not, because any tax you have already paid will be deducted from the total that you owe for the year. We'll see exactly how in the example figures at the end of this chapter.

Does all money coming in count as income?

Alex also needs to keep in mind while doing their freelance book-keeping that *all money coming in* is income, including:

- Reimbursements for expenses from producers.

- Touring allowance, per diems ('per diem', which is Latin for 'by the day', is a fancy term beloved of producers and agents that simply means an agreed daily sum intended to be an allowance for food and other living expenses incurred while at work), expense payments for travel, etc.

- The part of their fee that they never actually received because their agent kept it as commission. Alex does not ignore this, they account for it. Their fee is the *gross* fee, and the agent commission is an *expense*.

- Pension contributions made by an engager. This is much misunderstood, and needs some care. Many creative engagements feature two kinds of pension contribution: the 'employee' and the 'employer' contributions. 'Employee contribution' means that Alex agrees to have £50 of his £1,000 fee deducted from his earnings and put into a pension plan for them (we'll discuss more about how this works in Chapter 5). This does not affect the amount of income Alex declares – they still declare it all, as if the deduction had not been made. 'Employer contribution' means that the engager gives Alex some additional money, over and above the agreed fee, for their pension pot. Alex needs to remember to add this amount to the fee that they declare as taxable (although there may be an additional tax relief on it later – to be discussed in Chapter 5).

'Cash accounting' vs. 'accrual accounting'

This is accountant-speak to answer the question, 'When do I account for the fees I receive?'

Many people doing their own tax return are likely to find that they pause to ask themselves, 'When should I account for the income from a job I did on 30 March, but which I didn't get paid for until 10 April? Does it belong to the old year or the new year?'

I am sorry to tell you that the answer is… it depends. First, let's get clear on the two different accounting concepts that are the foundation of the answer: cash and accrual accounting.

'Cash accounting' means that you account for money *at the time a payment changed hands*.

'Accrual accounting' (sometimes called 'traditional accounting') means, by contrast, that you account for money at the time to which it belongs for a reason *other than because it changed hands*. This might be, for example, the date that the supplier invoiced the client; or it may be the date that the work was actually done.

Say for example that a painter and decorator spends three months decorating my house, from 1 March to 31 May. We agree that she will invoice me half at the start of the job and half at the end, and that I have two weeks to pay each invoice.

She can choose to do cash accounting, meaning that she will account for half the fee on 15 March and half on 14 June, being the dates that I paid.

Or she can choose accrual accounting. Under accrual accounting, it would be reasonable for her *either* to account for half on 1 March and half on 31 May, because those are the dates on her invoices; *or* in *three* parts, the first on 31 March, the second on 30 April and the third on 31 May, because that is a fair reflection of when the work was done.

Notice two things about the accrual accounting method: first, the date of her actual receipt of the cash is irrelevant; and second, that the choice of method alters the amount of tax payable in each of the two tax years concerned. Under cash accounting, and under the first accrual method, the entire fee is taxed evenly in two parts. But under the second accrual example, one-third is taxed in the earlier year and two-thirds in the later year.

This may well not matter at all, in the scheme of things. But that depends. Suppose that the painter had a bumper year in Year One, but a poor year by comparison in Year Two. It may then work to her advantage to have used the second accrual example, to push more income into a year in which she may be taxed at basic rate rather than leave it in a year in which she is taxed at higher rate.

None of these three methods is the single 'right', or required method. It is up to you, as the owner of your business, to choose the method that you believe gives the truest and fairest picture (and in practice you can make a case for 'true and fair' in a huge variety of ways).

The online tax return form defaults to the cash method (NB. It was the other way round until 2024/25), unless you tick the box to select accrual or 'traditional' accounting.

You can't, in practice, chop and change between methods from year to year. One change at one point is fine from the method you started with, although you need to be clear about why you have introduced it.

The advent of Making Tax Digital does not change the question about whether to use the cash basis or the accrual basis. Unfortunately this is likely to cause additional confusion about how income and expenditure fits in to MTD quarterly updates, especially if you are doing them yourself, but you are free, counterintuitive though it may seem, to make quarterly updates on the accrual basis if you wish.

I generally advise creative industry workers to use the accrual basis and to use dates on invoices and receipts as accounting dates, except on occasions when there has been a significant delay between work being done and invoice being sent. I say this because:

i. It's usually easier, especially for those working through an agent who sends out invoices once a week.

ii. It's generally a truer and fairer representation of the working life of a creative person.

iii. It offers more flexibility when unusual things have happened, to make a case for accounting for them in one period or another; this flexibility is lost to those using the cash basis, which always only ever means one thing – the date you got the money.

iv. If you have received a grant and need to defer some of it, this can only be done with the accruals basis (we discuss this further next).

Other kinds of income

Grant income and deferrals... and accrual accounting

Over the past few years it has become more common for creative freelancers to apply for and receive grants from the Arts Council and other funders to support relatively small projects, or to undertake R&D on new projects.

A grant of this kind will usually be taxable income in the hands of the recipient. If Alex applies for and receives a grant of £10,000, they will be liable to pay tax on that. But of course Alex would expect to incur considerable costs with that money; for example, to pay the other freelancers working on the project with them, and for physical production costs such as costumes and equipment hires. These costs – these expenses – will all be deductions against the £10,000, for tax purposes.

Say, then, that Alex spends £8,000 of the £10,000 on costs like this, and keeps only the surplus of £2,000 for themselves, to pay themselves while carrying out the project. This means they will be taxed on the £2,000, exactly as if the £2,000 had been a fee paid to them by another producer.

Sometimes a freelancer will receive such a grant in one tax year but not spend it until the following year. Say that this happened to Alex. They received the grant in March, but the project will not begin till September (they couldn't go ahead, after all, until they knew they had the money).

If you've been reading closely, you will now spot that Alex has a problem if they use the *cash* basis for accounting. They are obliged to pay tax *on the whole £10,000*, because they've received it in March. This is why it is critical, if you receive grants, to use the *accrual* method.

There are one or two other technicalities in this manoeuvre which are tricky to get watertight if you are doing your return by yourself, but if Alex wants to do that on this occasion, they need to keep in mind that they have here by default decided on an accounting system which they are going to have to stick to. Their projects are accounted for *in the year in which they actually happen, regardless of when the cash was received.* This then means that the £10,000 does not need to be reported when it is received, but in the *following* year.

As long as Alex ticks the right boxes on the return, and is consistent about that system from year to year, then this is fine, because it is quite clearly a reasonable and fair system for a producer to have.

Slightly different provisions apply to the type of grants called 'Developing Your Creative Practice' (DYCP) grants from the Arts Council. These are sometimes not taxable at all. You will need specialist advice about your particular case if you have received one of these grants.

Pension income

We will discuss pensions more fully in Chapter 5, but for now let's simply note that pension income is taxable income, so if you get it, you declare it on your tax return and include it in your tax calculation. The State Pension does not have tax taken off at source, so if you owe tax on it, you must pay that through your self-assessment return. Private pensions often do have tax deducted at source, but you need to compile and report the exact figures because if you receive, say, a couple of pensions and still work a bit too, it is highly unlikely that the correct amount will have been deducted at source, and you will need to include your figures in the tax return process to ensure there has been no underpayment or overpayment.

Renting out rooms in a property you own

Let's move on to issues that surround owning property and paying tax on income you make from it.

Income from renting property has to be reported and is taxable on the landlord – i.e. the landlord has to pay tax on it – when it is more than £1,000 per year.

Landlords, like the self-employed, are required to register for self-assessment and declare and pay tax on rental profits every year.

As we have seen, the self-assessment tax return is a snapshot of all income for the year, regardless of source, so a landlord reports their property income and tax as well as all their employment or self-employment earnings, all on the same return.

Landlords are allowed to deduct the costs of renting their property out (e.g. agents' fees, insurance, repairs, safety checks, etc.) from the rental income, before paying tax on the profit (the income minus the allowable expenses).

If landlords are paying a mortgage on the property that they rent out, then although the mortgage interest is not a deductible expense, tax relief fixed at 20% is given for it on the tax return, so this does work out as an additional advantage.

These provisions do not usually apply to lodgers. The process I just described generally only relates to a situation where you rent out an entire, separate property (i.e. it's got its own front door). Lodgers are usually dealt with under the 'Rent-A-Room' provision. Under this provision, you pay no tax on the first £7,500 of rent (£3,750 if you own the property jointly) and do not deduct any expenses; you just pay tax on any rent over £7,500.

Rental income counts towards the threshold for liability to join MTD. If you have self-employment income of £40,000 and rental income of £10,000, then you are in the first cohort for MTD in 2026/27 and your quarterly updates need to include your rental figures as well as your self-employment figures.

If you have expenses for building work and renovations, you might ask if these are deductible against rental income. Some types of renovations will be allowable; others will not be, but may then be allowable as a deduction for Capital Gains Tax (more on CGT below) when the property is sold. Landlords will usually need specialist advice to get this right.

Charitable and family gifts

Amounts that you are awarded from charitable foundations because you are in financial hardship (as opposed to grants that fund arts activity), and gifts from close relatives or life-partners, will almost always not be considered 'business income' and are therefore not taxable and do not need to be stated on your return.

If you receive gifts from close relatives who subsequently die within seven years, then the gift may well be treated as liable to Inheritance Tax, to be paid by the estate of the deceased person. This provision exists to stop parents simply giving all their money to their children towards the end of their lives in order to avoid Inheritance Tax. Bear this in mind if you receive a significantly sized gift from comparatively wealthy and comparatively elderly relatives; it can lead to complex situations.

Student loans – back to thresholds

Alex took a student loan while they were studying. When you receive a student loan payment, it is not taxable income. But you do need to think about how it is paid back; Alex becomes liable to start paying it back in any year in which their income goes over a certain threshold. Student loan repayments can be deducted from PAYE, or made through the self-assessment tax return, or (less commonly) paid directly to Student Finance (but don't set this up unless there is a reason why you are not doing one of the other two).

The threshold depends on the type and timing of the original loan, and it changes every year, but it is generally a little under £30,000 per year. Alex will usually repay 9% of the part of their income which is over the threshold, so if they earned £35,000 gross in a year, they owe 9% x 5,000 = £450 for the year.

Student loan repayments are in effect an extra tax, although those who never reach the earnings threshold will never be liable to pay them.

Capital Gains Tax (CGT)

Until now, we have been discussing the UK's income tax regime, that's to say the way it taxes earnings and rental income. There are some other important types of tax. We'll come on to VAT later, but here I want to talk about Capital Gains Tax.

The UK also taxes capital gains, which are increases in the value of assets. Say that Alex bought some shares in a big company for £100 because they had once heard it was a good investment. Two years later, the shares have increased in value to £200. Alex has made a gain of £100 and, if they sell the shares at that point, they will be liable to CGT on the £100.

Different rates of CGT apply to different types of assets. There is generally a small annual threshold below which no CGT is payable if you have only had a couple of small gains.

The most common scenarios in which CGT is payable are:

i. You hold shares and decide to sell them.

ii. You have savings funds in, for example, unit trusts or a stocks-and-shares portfolio, and even though you don't pay any attention to them because they are your 'rainy day' savings, the bank sends you a statement every year setting out your gains and losses in the year.

iii. You buy and sell cryptocurrencies.

iv. You sell a property that you did not live in; for example, a property you were renting out. (No CGT is payable when you sell the one property that you actually live in.) This is the only common circumstance in which you have to make a special CGT return and pay any tax due within two months of the property sale.

If you made a capital *loss* in a year, then it is also always important to report this on your return, because it is carried forward to offset against whatever gain you may make in a future year.

Most creative freelancers do not report capital gains in most years but if you do, again, it is probably necessary to take bespoke advice to get it completely correct in your case.

Inheritance Tax

In the UK, the estate of a deceased person is sometimes taxed, if it is over a certain threshold. Inheritance Tax is paid by the estate before bequests are passed to the beneficiaries. Therefore, if you receive money from the estate of someone who has died, you do not generally have to pay any tax on it; either no tax was due, or it has been paid by the estate during the probate process before you receive it.

If, however, you receive assets from an estate, such as a property or jewellery, then you may well be liable to Capital Gains Tax in future, when you sell these assets, by paying tax on the gain you have made from the time that the bequest was made to you up to the time that you sell the asset. So it's important to have any asset that you receive as a bequest valued professionally and recorded, at the time that you receive it.

Paying the tax owed

We've now considered all the different types of income which Alex has received, so it's time to dive into the mechanism and calculations for their first return and payments.

Payment on account

Payment on account, which would be better termed 'Tax Payments Up Front', is a rather complex, confusing and cumbersome mechanism that HMRC uses to stagger their receipt of all the tax that arrives via self-assessment. If you have done self-assessment before and have struggled to get your head round this concept, you are in very good company.

We have discussed that your payment deadline for a tax year is ten months after the end of that year – 31 January 2027 for the year that began on 6 April 2025 and ended on 5 April 2026. (See page 23 to remind yourself.)

So if Alex shoots a huge ad on 7 April 2025 with a fee of £50,000, they will not owe their approximately £15,000 of tax and NIC on that until nearly two years later, on 31 January 2027. You can understand how the State wants a mechanism whereby at least some of that money arrives earlier, so that it can spend it on hospitals, the Navy, and redecorating 10 Downing Street. Hence the payment on account mechanism. It is a blunt tool for the State to get its hands on some of Alex's tax earlier.

Under payment on account, the first time Alex goes over a £1,000 tax bill for a year, the system will make them pay not only the tax due for the *historical* year, but also *the same again up front for next year* – half on 31 January and half on 31 July.

If Alex then magically earned exactly the same amount year after year, they would subsequently always make exactly the same payment on 31 January and 31 July every year, until they get to the last ever year of business, before retirement. In that year there would (hooray) be no tax to pay because Alex would already have paid it up front. (Alex must remember to retire before they die, or this benefit will be entirely wasted.)

Alex's friend Shobu explains her own liability for 2024/25 to Alex, in this context:

> Shobu earned about £20,000 profit in 2024/25 and let's say her tax and NI bill for 2024/25 is £2,000.
>
> It's the first time Shobu has had a tax bill of more than £1,000, and so on 31 January 2026, she pays not only that £2,000 but *also half of it again* – £1,000 on account – a total payment of £3,000.
>
> On 31 July 2026, she pays the other £1,000 on account.
>
> If Shobu made exactly the same profit every year after that, she would always then simply pay £1,000 every January and £1,000 every July (except that in reality, of course she doesn't, so these numbers will go up and down every year).

One of the main ways in which HMRC make this far more complicated than necessary is that the amount shown as payable at the bottom of your annual tax calculation *does not take account of amounts you have already paid on account*. In the above example, Shobu's 2025/26 calculation will state at the bottom that she owes £2,000 whereas in fact she only owes £1,000, because she's already paid £1,000 on account.

We discussed above that even though the deadline for a tax return is 31 January, it is perfectly possible to file much earlier, say in May or June of the previous year, very soon after the end of the tax year. Once you are in the payment on account system, it becomes an even better idea to file early in the year, say in May or June – because then, if the 31 July payment is set too high, it is adjusted down before you actually pay it.

What happens if my income is much lower this year than it was last year?

We can see that if your income always stays exactly the same then the payment on account system is perfect. And if your income increases every year, you owe a bit more when you reach the end of the year, but your payment on account has been quite a helpful mechanism because it means you have paid most of your bill upfront and don't need to find the cash again.

But if your income decreases or, more likely as a freelancer, fluctuates unpredictably, then there could be a problem here. You might well then be being asked to pay more on account than you actually owe, because the payment on account is being based on last year's figures, not this year's.

Therefore, at the point of filing your next return, there is some scope to reduce the payment on account if you think you have made significantly lower income in the new year so far, than you did in the previous year. You claim to reduce your new payment on account, on your next return.

There *is* an element of risk in claiming a reduction of payment on account. If you underestimate what you should pay on account, and then it turns out that your tax bill is higher and you were wrong, HMRC will charge interest on the portion that is unpaid. That said: the interest rate is low, the amount which may have been underestimated is low, and you can always mitigate the risk by filing early, say in May or June, which means that the period on which any interest may be due is short.

Unfortunately you are between a rock and a hard place here – you can't be certain, so sticking to the calculated figure necessarily runs the opposite risk: that of paying more on 31 January than you strictly need to, and then having to wait till next year's filing to get any overpayment back.

This is in effect quite a good free test of individual psychology. Some people are keen to avoid the risk of underpaying and always stick to the calculated figure; others hate the idea of paying too much up-front, and so are willing to risk claiming a reduction even if there is the chance of having to pay some interest.

The 'Time to Pay' scheme

It is always best to try to pay your tax bill on time, or you may well incur interest and penalties. Below we will analyse, in Alex's full tax calculation for the year, a method you can use to estimate your tax bill as you go along; and it is best to set aside what you think you will have to pay in a savings account or other separate pot. But this isn't always possible, and you can find that you end up with a bill you can't pay. For this reason, HMRC has a discretionary mechanism to allow taxpayers to pay their tax in instalments if they did not set aside sufficient sums to pay their tax bill as they went along.

In these circumstances, it is always best to apply to HMRC's 'Time to Pay' scheme, rather than just leave things and fall behind with payments – that will generate a string of nasty letters from HMRC and worse, sooner or later they will pass your case to commercial debt collectors. With apologies to any commercial debt collectors reading this, these are folks with whom all professional contact is best avoided throughout your life, whatever the circumstances.

You can usually apply for 'Time to Pay' online, or HMRC advertise a special phone number to call. Almost all requests are agreed, provided that you have not fallen behind with payments before and provided you are ready to make sensible proposals about the schedule of payments. Interest will be added to these, but this is all agreed and communicated to you in advance, so it's a much better position than being left uncertain about what you owe; or borrowing the money commercially, or going overdrawn at the bank in order to pay HMRC. These methods are likely to work out much more expensive and uncertain; so if you are in this position, get ahead of the game as soon as you can and set up a 'Time to Pay' plan.

Non-UK nationals and dual citizens – also known as: where do we pay tax?

Some background on Alex and their flatmates:

Alex is a UK citizen who has lived in the UK all their life, whereas

- Jo is a Hungarian national living in the UK with Indefinite Leave to Remain.
- Sam, meanwhile, was born in the USA and moved to the UK a few years ago. Sam is a dual UK-US citizen.

Alex only has reporting and tax obligations in the UK, thank goodness. However, in this globalised world of ours, there is often enormous confusion about the position of those like Jo and Sam. Let's try to break this down and establish some principles that are easy to follow.

As a rule, you report and pay tax *only where you live*. Most of the time, your nationality is irrelevant to tax on your work earnings, and so is the currency that you were paid in, and the geographical location of the bank that you were paid to. Often, creatives who are working in countries A and B intuitively think they should pay their tax on earnings in A in A, and their tax on earnings in B in B. I understand why they think this, but they are usually wrong.

There are four main exceptions to keep in mind:

i. If you have income from **property**, for example because you own a house or flat that you rent out, then this will almost always be taxed first in the country where the property is, regardless of where you yourself live.

ii. The **USA** is almost the only country in the world that requires all its citizens to file a tax return, even if they don't live in the USA, even if they are also citizens of another country, and even if they don't have any tax to pay in the USA.

iii. It is possible to be a **dual resident** – this means more than one country regards you as tax resident and liable to report, and possibly pay, taxes. This usually happens because you are spending a significant chunk of time, repeatedly, in more than one country. A complex system of bilateral agreements between most pairs of countries in the world exists, which sets out in very long, very boring but very important detail what those two countries have agreed about which one you should pay your taxes to. It depends on which countries they are, how you got the money on which tax is due, and often lots of other factors too.

iv. It often happens when a UK resident does some work overseas that **the employer or engager withholds some money** to pay tax on those earnings in that country. Either this has been done correctly, and we'll explain what happens in consequence later, or it has been done incorrectly, in which case the UK resident has some work to do to reclaim the tax in the other country.

Assuming that Jo is living and working in London, and, let's say, returning to Hungary only for a few weeks of the year, for holidays and visiting friends and family, she will not have any reporting or tax obligation in Hungary, but only in the UK.

Sam, by contrast, *does* have a reporting obligation in the USA, even if all his work and income has been in the UK, because of the unusual rules of the USA. Assuming all his income and work was in the UK then he does not owe any actual tax in the USA, and can simply make a 'nil' return, probably without even engaging an accountant in the USA.

Unless Jo or Sam have income from *property* in the country they are not resident in, it is most unlikely that they will have to pay any tax in that country, even if they did some work there during the year.

This area can get complicated though, so if Jo or Sam were in any doubt about this, they would be wise to seek the advice of an accountant. In this situation, my earlier advice about only using arts-specialist accountants is particularly important. This is because the rules that govern how to work out which country tax is due in, when a resident of one country works in another, are often different for work in the creative industries and sports to the rules for other professions.

Working out where you are tax-resident, and whether you are resident in more than one country in a tax year, can be a very difficult and complicated matter when you spend a good deal of time in more than one country. Without going into all the rules here, let us note that a common misconception is that you are tax-resident *only* in the country where you spent more than 183 days of the year (i.e. the majority of the year). There is much more to it than that, so if you are in doubt about these areas, you need bespoke advice.

As it happens, Jo did one job overseas in the year – she was in a touring show that spent six weeks in Italy. Jo received a letter from the producer explaining that the Italian producing partners, who were paying the company wages in Italy, would be deducting tax at source, and indeed this was what happened, as was clear from Jo's payslips.

This deduction is correct under the terms of the tax treaty between the UK and Italy. Jo is in all probability entitled to a Foreign Tax Credit in the UK when she comes to complete her UK self-assessment, so that the tax she paid in Italy will be *deducted* from the tax she owes in the UK. The principle there is simple, but the methodology is quite tricky, and Jo may struggle to fill in the tax return correctly by herself insofar as it relates to this aspect.

A further complication arising from the Italy gig is the National Insurance Contributions (NIC) position.

Jo may have been advised to complete and send a form to HMRC which is often called an 'A1' form (although this is a historical anomaly – the actual A1 form is long dead, but everyone still calls it an 'A1'. Now it's a C-3-8-something-or-other in some circumstances, and other versions in others). An A1 form tells an overseas engager that a UK resident does not have to pay social security contributions in the country where the work is done. This advice to Jo typically comes from any of three sources:

i. Alex's friend Bob did a job overseas three years ago, remembers that he had to 'fill in an A1', and mentions this to Alex who mentions it to Jo.

ii. Jo's agent routinely 'completes A1s whenever their clients work overseas'.

iii. The Italian producer 'asked Jo to submit an A1' and to send them the certificate that HMRC send back.

The last of these is really the only reason that we would advise Jo to go ahead and complete the A1. For a job of only a few weeks, it is not otherwise really worth her going to the trouble.

A common misconception is that the A1 is necessary in order to avoid being taxed twice: this is not true. Jo in fact avoids double taxation through the Foreign Tax Credit process we discussed above.

The A1 simply avoids some NIC being paid twice, but for a short job, this is likely to be very small amounts and it is uncertain that the A1 can arrive in time to stop the deductions being made anyway.

If, however, the overseas engager *requires* the form, Jo has little choice but to complete and send it. The producer is doing this to help themselves, not Jo – *they* will pay lower employer taxes in their home country if the process is followed.

For a job of several *months* overseas, we would advise Jo to complete an A1 in any case, because then there may well be a worthwhile saving in their NIC for the year.

Working on cruise ships

Alex has not (yet) done any work on cruise ships; but their friend Camilla has, straight from college. She has become part of the almost naval force of entertainers who staff the unbelievably large theatres on these floating palaces. Let us briefly discuss the position here, around which, again, many common misconceptions arise.

It is not true that all work on cruise ships is tax-free. Some such work sometimes is, in some circumstances. This can get complicated, and so here, again, Camilla may well need advice from a theatre-specialist accountant.

Camilla's contract on a cruise ship will *either* be one of self-employment *or* employment. If it is self-employment, then it is unlikely that this will be treated and taxed differently to any other self-employment work, unless her time away forms part of several years outside the UK. The work will be part of her UK self-employment business, just as if she had done any other type of UK tour.

Some *employment* on ships, by contrast, *is* exempt from tax under a provision called 'Seafarers' Entitlement'. This exemption applies if Camilla's voyage is long enough, without lengthy breaks when she was back in the UK. If she has cruise contracts that span more than one year, then this is well worth looking at. It is also vital to consider it in advance if Camilla has cruise jobs booked more than a few months ahead, *before* embarking on a cruise of more than about six months; because with advance planning she might be able to plan and execute an itinerary that allows her to qualify for the exemption. It's easy to overlook this and only to think about it once she has already been back in the UK for a while, by which time (sorry) the ship has sailed (I'm here all week).

If Camilla does qualify for the exemption, and if she has planned a strategy sufficiently in advance, then she will make a tax return at the end of a tax year in which she claims the Seafarers' Entitlement. This will lead to a refund of any tax that she paid in that employment. It will also potentially have a positive impact on her overall tax position for the year.

Correcting errors on returns already submitted

If you discover an error on a tax return you have already submitted, you are usually liable to file an amendment. This can be done online within twelve months of the deadline for submitting the return, or by post thereafter.

There is a longstanding convention that if an error on an income tax return has caused a mistaken effect of up to £200 in tax – so if the error has caused you to pay up to £200 either too much or too little – then an amendment is not required. You should simply make an adjustment to the same value on your *next* return. Bear in mind that this convention doesn't apply to VAT – this is dealt with differently, so more on this later.

Alex's forecast tax calculation, and how much they should have saved as they went along

Armed with our knowledge of the tax system, we can now make an estimate of Alex's tax calculation for the 2025/26 year. Ideally, they should have had a go at this when they first started work in August 2025; the figures would, of course, be very rough at that stage, but doing the exercise gives Alex at least some idea of how much they need to save in order not to have a nasty surprise when the time comes to pay any tax due in January 2027.

Alex's income in 2025/26 (having graduated in August 2025, up to 31 March 2026)

	£
Casual shifts in Lauren's shop (PAYE)	10,000
Tour of *Sleeping Beauty* (including travel and per diem payments from producer)	5,000
Three days as Nurse #375 in *Casualty*	1,200

Work with Alex's friend's roleplay company	2,000
Kids' guitar lessons	1,000
Rehearsals (March) for tour of *Innit!* opening in April	1,600
TOTAL income	**20,800**

First, a pat on the back to Alex – they've succeeded in making a little bit more than we calculated in Chapter 1 that they would need to survive.

We'll discuss expenses in much more detail in the next chapter, but for now let's say that Alex has had £2,000 of allowable expenses for their acting business.

Therefore their taxable income for the year is:

£20,800 - £2,000 = £18,800

Remember that Alex needs to think of three types of payment:

i. Tax

ii. National Insurance

iii. Student loan

Alex's *tax* bill for the year is calculated after subtracting the personal allowance:

£18,800 - £12,570 = £6,230 x 20% = £1,246

Alex now looks at the P60 received from Lauren in the shop and deducts from the tax bill any PAYE tax that had already been deducted by Lauren when she paid the shop wages – otherwise they would be paying that tax twice. As it happened, Lauren deducted £200 in total, so Alex's tax bill goes down to £1,046.

Their *National Insurance* bill for the year is £0, because they have self-employment profits of £10,800 - £2,000 = £8,800, which is below the threshold for Class 4 NICs. Alex has successfully 'clocked up' a Full Year of work towards their State Pension, by virtue of both their shop work and their self-employment. This will be marked automatically on Alex's NI record after the return is submitted.

Their *student loan* bill for the year is also £0, because they are under the student loan repayment income threshold of about £30,000.

Starting with the £1,046, we now remember that Alex will be brought into the payment on account system (see page 62), because £1,046 is more than £1,000. So on 31 January 2027 Alex will pay:

2025/26 tax: £1,046

Payment on account part one (half again): £523

Making a 31 January 2027 total bill of: £1,569

On 31 July 2027 Alex will pay the second payment on account of £523. If they always earned exactly the same amounts in future, they would pay £523 every January and every July until retirement.

If Alex estimates this when starting work in August 2025, they will calculate that they should put into savings approximately £200 per month from the start. That will provide a savings cushion of approximately £1,600 by April 2026, which as we can see will cover the January 2027 bill.

Important rule-of-thumb for how much to save as you go along

Alex was earning, on average, £20,000 ÷ 8 months = £2,500 per month, so the £200 per month that I suggest saving for taxes represents about 8% of this. At this level of earnings, saving 8%-10% of what you are earning monthly should be enough to cover you. You should think of increasing that to 15% or even 20% when you start to get much better-paid jobs which will take you over the Class 4 NI, student loan and eventually higher-rate tax thresholds.

★ ★ ★

Well done, Alex! In the next chapter, let's look in greater detail at the question of Alex's *expenses* and exactly how they arrived at that figure for deductions of £2,000.

Golden rules for income

- Your tax return is not just for your freelance income, it's for any PAYE income too.

- Most creatives should use the accrual ('traditional') accounting method, not the cash accounting method.

- Do not assume rules about overseas tax – check your particular situation.

- Get your head round the payment on account mechanism and always save up as you go along for the tax bill of the future.

4. Tax and Expenses

General observations

'Expenses' as a subject raises quite a few issues for taxpayers (especially freelance creatives), accountants, and HMRC, and it's worth spending a while taking a look at them here.

The principle is simple: a business is not taxed on its income but on its profits; that is to say, its income minus its expenses.

In general, there is never much question about defining income, because your engagers – your 'customers' – paid you what they paid you. Expenses are much harder to define.

The law states that expenses for a business are allowable when they are 'wholly and exclusively incurred' for the purpose of running your business.

If that were all there was to it, life would be very simple. You would claim a deduction only for those expenses which were only ever spent, and entirely spent, on your business.

But think about what this would mean in reality. You would need two pencils on your desk at all times, one of which you only ever used for work and did claim the cost of, and the other of which you used for writing notes to family members, for which you did not claim the cost.

In reality, of course, people do not behave like this. It's an important 'of course', because there is something here about really doing business in a real world that we all agree exists, and therefore something importantly 'human' embedded in tax law. People do not have two pencils, one for work and one for family – and nor do tribunal judges expect them to.

The daily life of creative industry workers (and many other kinds of self-employed people) is characterised by little or no separation between the timing and manner of tasks done for the business, and those done for personal or leisure purposes. And so, in practice, a system of understanding how to categorise your expenses is needed, which at times can seem rather more complex than it merits.

Why does all this matter? There are two answers: one financial and one moral.

Financial

The higher the expenses you state, the less tax you pay. Let's say Alex decides to take their agent out for a nice lunch, believing that if such a lunch takes place, the agent will be more likely to get Alex more and better auditions (Alex is probably wrong about that, but never mind – it's something actors sometimes think).

The lunch costs £100. If Alex can claim that it is 'allowable', or 'deductible' (these words mean the same thing in this context), they will pay between £20 and £54 less tax and NI at the end of the year, than if they do not claim it is allowable/deductible – because tax on income is reduced by the amount of allowable expenses.

The result of this financial fact is that many self-employed people take time and trouble to ensure that they have maximised their statement of allowable expenses, in order to minimise their tax bill. Which brings us to:

Moral

Is this morally legitimate behaviour? After all, your taxes (mostly) pay for great things for all of us – hospitals, public transport, schools, benefits. Shouldn't right-thinking creative industry people be trying to pay as much tax as they can, to support the community?

I have no hesitation in answering an unequivocal, absolute 'no' to this last question, for two reasons:

First, the way to think about these matters most fairly is to 'play by the rules', not to try to rewrite them. You aren't required to decide what is or isn't fair in morality, but only what did or did not happen in fact. Parliament and the law have done the former for you, to the best of their ability. It is often hard to interpret what they mean, but that is what you should try to do, rather than focus on the broader question of 'whether you are paying your way in society'. If you feel guilty that you aren't, give some money to a charity, which will usually spend it more wisely than the State.

Second, you can be sure that large companies retain full-time, in-house accountants much cleverer than me who spend their entire working lives trying to maximise their expenses and minimise the company's tax bill. If you don't apply the same philosophy on a smaller scale to your own business, you are just taking more of the tax burden (proportionally) on your shoulders than they are, and this is manifestly unfair.

Nobody disputes that this area is difficult; but you make both a financial and moral mistake if you do not engage with it seriously, and as a result either cheat and pay too little tax, or conversely, understate your expenses and pay too much tax. The proper way is the only correct way – and ultimately it is the only defensible way.

* * *

If you have earned more than £90,000 income in a year, the tax return requires you to divide up and report your expenses in various standard categories, e.g. travel, marketing, office costs, etc. If you have earned below that threshold, you do not need to do this, and you can simply report one figure for your total expenses.

Unfortunately, intuitive thinking about which expenses are deductible is only useful up to a point. For example, you might intuitively think that the cost of reading glasses is deductible, since you would be unable to read scripts without them. Perhaps scripts are the only things you really read, and so you use your glasses pretty much exclusively for work. But this is incorrect. As we will discuss later on, the cost of reading glasses is not deductible (though the cost of contact lenses for an actor probably is – more on this anomaly later). Your intuition about these matters only takes you so far, and you need the guidance in this chapter to help you come to a more robust view.

And perhaps you have been wondering about that agent lunch, since I mentioned it. The meal that Alex's agent ate is *not* deductible. The meal that *Alex* ate with their agent *might be*. Read on.

Trading allowance

Actually, the very first thing to note about expenses for tax is not really about expenses at all – it is about Trading Allowance.

Tax law gives every sole trader business an allowance of £1,000 expenses for which you do not have to provide any proof: it does not matter if these are deductible expenses or not. The rationale behind this is that i) it would be pretty difficult to run any business without incurring expenditure of about £1,000 per year, once you count your phone, computer, travel costs, stationery, etc.; and ii) it would never be worth HMRC's trouble to argue about expenses that add up to less than that.

So, if Alex adds up expenses for the year and they are less than £1,000, they do not write down the lower total on the tax return – they just tick the Trading Allowance box instead (Trading Allowance is an alternative to claiming expenses, not an addition) and then they have in effect claimed their statutory minimum £1,000.

I see this mistake again and again on tax returns that sole traders have filled in themselves. They have written down less than £1,000 expenses. This is just a waste of money, so now you know never to do it again.

Obviously allowable expenses

I generally advise that the list I'm about to show you details expenses which are, in almost all cases, uncontroversially allowable for many different kinds of creative industry workers – you hardly need even to think about these ones.

You obviously need to be aware of the relationship between the type of expense and your particular discipline within the creative domain. For example, an actor can deduct the cost of their haircuts, but a lighting designer cannot (the best lighting designers all have very long hair, anyway), even though both parties work in theatre. Conversely, you would expect a lighting designer to have higher IT costs than an actor, because they spend more work time doing more and different activities on their laptop.

Agent commission

Many people make the mistake of reporting income after commission from their agent has been taken off. They then ignore the commission amount altogether. This is wrong. Your income is your *gross* income *before* commission is taken off, and the commission should then be reported as an *expense*. This is because the agent has in effect cost you something.

So, if you earned a fee of £1,000 and your agent took 12.5% + VAT = £150, then you do not just write down income of £850. You write down income of £1,000 and an expense of £150. (NB. You do not include the VAT if you are VAT-registered, see Chapter 6.)

Travel

Almost everyone in this sector will have public transport expenses for work, and/or taxi fares, etc.

Use of private vehicles is more complicated – more on this on page 100.

See also below (page 102) for more analysis on the problem of travel between home and a venue that you go to *regularly*.

If you are obliged to pay for a visa to visit a country to which you are only going for work, then the cost is deductible – but see notes below on costs like passports, work-permit applications, etc., which are very unlikely to be deductible.

Printing, stationery and postage

Deduct the cost of that packet of pencils. Nobody minds that of course you will use one of the pencils for a personal matter, not a business matter, at some stage or other. It is normal, not illegal, to do this.

Also include obvious things like printing and posting out headshots.

IT running costs

For example, software charges, etc. – read on below (page 85) for more about larger equipment purchases.

Materials, resources, etc.

Sheet music, props, etc. that you supplied for yourself.

Training/workshops

The cost of Alex's original professional training, or university fee, is *not* deductible (if it was, everyone in every job could claim their tuition fees!); but after they start, all ad hoc classes, trainings, workshops, masterclasses, dance sessions, etc., which are for continuing professional development, *are* deductible.

Professional fees

Equity membership; subscriptions to relevant professional bodies; solicitors' fees – but be careful here because if the fees are covering anything with a personal aspect like citizenship or permission-to-work applications, these will not be allowable. The types of solicitors' fees that would be allowable would be, for example, if you have a work contract dispute with someone and take advice, or if you take a lease on a workshop space and ask a solicitor to check it over for you.

Bank charges; interest on loans, including, for example, Bounceback loan

If you have a business bank account, the fees are deductible. Many people will have taken out business loans such as a Bounceback loan during Covid – the interest on the loan is deductible although the (principal) loan repayment itself is not.

Books and newspapers

Your subscription to *The Stage*, a book of monologues for auditions, etc.

Marketing, e.g. website, headshots, Spotlight, IMDb, etc.

And any similar costs. You may well incur some of these costs before you register as a sole trader, while you are still studying; they are allowable as 'pre-trading expenses' on your first tax return.

Equipment: cameras, ring-lights, laptops, phones, yoga mats

For relatively inexpensive and wholly professional items, simply allow the whole lot.

Things get more complicated where the items are a) expensive and b) for mixed business and leisure use.

There may be a case to treat items worth some thousands of pounds as 'Capital Assets' and not ordinary expenditure. I tend not to go down this road for items like laptops, phones, or cameras worth up to say £2,000 – but beyond that, you may need to take some more advice on this point.

There's more on b) below, on page 93.

We also deal specifically with buying vehicles later, on page 100 (a whole other level of complexity).

Repairs

Batteries for Alex's ring-light, new soles for their tap shoes…

Accountancy

Your accountant's fee if you use one, and/or the cost of this book.

Obviously disallowable expenses

After you have read the long section beginning on page 87 about more complex areas that require some judgement and informed opinion, you will be better able to spot disallowable expenses.

Let's set this up, though, by talking about the funny press items that HMRC publish from time to time, where they try to make the taxpaying public smile with stories of items that people have tried to claim that are quite obviously disallowable.

Some of these include, for example:

i. Your golf club membership – this is not a 'networking' expense.

ii. Your partner's air fare to accompany you to your shoot in Thailand, on the grounds that it is unhealthy for your relationship for you to be apart for too long.

iii. Your application fee for a passport, because 'my old one had expired and I needed the new one in time for a job overseas'. Nope, sorry.

iv. Your lawyers' fees for your UK citizenship application, 'because I can't work without that'. Yes, but if that was allowable for you, it would be allowable for every single person in the UK workforce applying for citizenship (it isn't).

v. Childcare expenses. (There are some mechanisms for tax-free childcare which we will come to in Chapter 5, but the fees you may pay to childminders or babysitters are not allowable business expenses, or anyone in any job could claim them.)

vi. The fish tank strategically placed in your Zoom camera background, 'to make it look nice'.

The reason to start talking about 'complexity' in this way is that, by pointing to some slightly ludicrous extremes which everyone can agree are disallowed, we can start to build understanding about less clear items. And this understanding is important for actors and other freelance creatives because without it, things can feel very confusing, cause stress and guilt, and also cause people with multiple sources of income to underestimate what they can claim for, and thus leave themselves with a higher tax bill than they need to pay.

More complex expense areas

We now come to some areas which are much trickier. In the remainder of this chapter we will cover:

i. Expenses incurred trying to get work, but not succeeding.

ii. Surprisingly allowable expenses.

iii. Expenses where you can allow a proportion, but not all.

iv. Use of your home as your office.

v. Use of vehicles.

vi. Travel – when you often go to the same place.

vii. Health and wellbeing.

viii. Clothes and personal appearance.

ix. Subsistence and accommodation.

i. Expenses incurred trying to get work, but not succeeding

The obvious premise behind our discussion thus far is that a business with some or plenty of income coming in must have expended expenditure in order to achieve that income. Alex can't appear in a play at a theatre without incurring travel costs to get there.

As everyone working in the creative industries knows only too well, however, it is perfectly possible to have a period of time – sometimes a long period – where little or no income is coming in from creative gigs, even though you are trying your hardest to get them and incurring some expenses in doing so (headshots, travel to meetings, classes, Spotlight, casting-website subscriptions, haircuts, etc.).

So, is it okay to file a tax return on which you have wiped out most of your income on expenses? And going even further, could you in fact report a loss on your creative business, if you have gone a year without much or any income but still had all your expenses? And what does that mean for your taxes in that year?

The short answer is yes, this is okay. So long as you are genuinely trying to get creative gigs, and have a commercial purpose and belief which is driving your activities, there is no technical reason why you cannot spend more than you make. Tax law is considering what you have done as a person in business. It takes no view at all on whether you are a successful person in business or not. In order for an expense to have been allowably incurred in your business, what matters is how hard you are *trying* to get income – not whether you are *succeeding*.

So suppose Alex's year had looked a little different to the one we analysed at the end of Chapter 3.

Suppose they had:

- Not done any of the creative work we listed because none of it had been offered.

- Used the time instead for, say, £10,000-worth of additional shifts in Lauren's shop, since no creative work was coming in and they still had to survive, and the shop wages were taxed PAYE.

- Still incurred the £2,000 of expenses on acting, because Alex spent the same amounts looking for creative gigs when they were not working in the shop.

These circumstances are likely to produce a situation where Alex reports a *loss* on their acting business of £2,000 in the year, because they have had £2,000 of expenses and no income. Alex then has a choice either to use the loss to *relieve* some of the PAYE they have paid, and receive a refund of tax after submitting their self-assessment; or to 'bank' the loss and use it to offset future creative profits in future years. Accountants call this '*carrying forward*', which means that the loss is not used at this point in time, in its current year, but is taken forward in time and used in a future year.

Another point to note here is that the eligibility of an expense has nothing to do with the amount it cost, provided that cost has the correct reasonable market value.

What do I mean? Well, perhaps you intuitively think that you have a responsibility to keep your expenses down, so that you make more profits and pay more tax. In fact you have no such responsibility. Say you had an audition in Tottenham Court Road, immediately followed by a work meeting in Marble Arch. If you take a taxi, this is obviously wholly and exclusively for your business, because work was the only reason you were in those places at those times. So the expense is allowable. HMRC do not disallow it on the grounds that you could have got the Tube instead, and claimed a smaller amount.

It follows that if an economy-class air ticket is allowable for a particular trip, then so is a business-class one for the same trip.

But this does not mean that Kim, a Korean friend of Alex's who does not pay tax in the UK because he is only visiting London, can sell Alex a pencil for £1,000 by agreement between them, so that Alex can get £200 off their tax bill – because £1,000 is not reasonable market value for a pencil.

ii. Surprisingly allowable expenses

I generally advise that creative industry workers can deduct the following expenses, and I find that this advice can cause some surprise because some people (and quite a few non-specialist accountants...) might intuitively disagree.

Paid-for content

For example, Netflix subscription, other paid-for TV, paid-for music, theatre and cinema tickets.

I advise that most creative industry workers will be entitled to claim all these costs. You may see some HMRC posts on the internet telling you that you can only claim these costs if they are relevant to your work. What they mean is, for example, that an actor who was only available for *theatre* work could claim their theatre tickets but not their *cinema* tickets. After thirty-five years in the industry I have yet to meet that person!

Subsistence and accommodation on an unusual day

'Subsistence' is fancy HMRC-speak for 'food and drink'.

Of all the types of expenses that I consider in my day-to-day work, this type causes the most confusion and the most difficulty.

It is a complex and technical area in tax, and it's impossible to come to a hard-and-fast, one-size-fits-all conclusion on it.

In one tribunal case on this matter, the judge said that the circumstances of different self-employed people in relation to this question are 'infinitely variable'.

So, on the one hand, absolutely everybody incurs these costs at some stage and therefore has to come to a view on it; but, on the other hand, if you asked two accountants about it, you'd get two different answers.

My usual starting point is to ask my clients to consider these two rules of thumb:

i. Were your circumstances on that day 'routine' or not? If you were somewhere that you don't routinely or normally go for work, then generally these expenses will be allowable. For example: I am typing this sentence at my office. If I now go round the corner and buy a coffee at the local café, it will not be deductible, because I am usually at my office. But if I decide that tomorrow I will go to the British Library to look up some things I need to check for this book, I will claim the cost of the coffee I buy in their lovely café, because I only rarely go and work at the British Library.

ii. I find that it is often useful to ask yourself – was the *travel* to the place where I bought the food allowable? It will generally follow that if it was, then the food itself is allowable, and vice versa.

We consider some of these questions in a bit more detail in our discussion on the Tim Healy tribunal case on page 124, below. You cannot normally allow subsistence for other people, which explains why Alex can't deduct the cost of their agent's lunch.

Contact lenses

Why are contact lenses allowable when glasses are not?

On the one hand, there is a general principle that expenses connected to your health are *not* allowable.[*] Yes, your good health helps you work, but it also helps you do everything else.

On the other hand, an actor's appearance is obviously a critical tool for use in their business. You cannot have headshots that show you without glasses, if in fact you need glasses to be able to do anything on stage or on a set.

So if contact lenses are your solution to the challenge of maintaining your appearance as an actor or model, they must be allowable.

---

[*] We will discuss the area of health and wellbeing in more detail on page 105.

iii. Expenses where you can allow a proportion, but not all

Hang on a minute. We said above that an expense had to be 'wholly' incurred for business in order to be allowable. So how can there be a concept of taking a proportion or a percentage of an expense? If something needs to be split to be allowed, then surely it isn't 'wholly' allowable, by definition?

Yet... hang on another minute. If there isn't such a concept, what do you do about, for example, your phone, which of course you use for a work call one minute and a personal call the next? Does tax law require you to have two phones?!

Of course it does not. Remember that tax law is connected to what real, reasonable people really, reasonably do. Welcome to the wonderful paradox of proportioning expenses, where tax law gets to have its cake and eat it, by saying that there are some expenses which are wholly and exclusively for your business, even when they are not wholly and exclusively for your business. Accountancy meets quantum physics.

In practice, of course, nobody wants to carry round two phones, two tablets, and two laptops. And it would be completely absurd for Alex to hop on the Tube to the West End for a casting call, then go back to Hoxton, and then go all the way back to the West End to meet their friend Ollie, in order to create one Tube journey which is allowable and one which is not. And so tax law has managed to establish a mechanism for dealing with the challenge of proportioning expenses.

Tax law says: 'If the expenditure can be apportioned reasonably accurately then the private element is disallowed.' Great. So if Alex can come up with a 'reasonably accurate' way of splitting the shared expense, they can allow the business part and disallow the personal part.

Fine word, 'reasonably'. How do we apply it in practice? Where is 'the man [sic] on the Clapham Omnibus' when you need him? (Apart from en-route to any of South London's wonderful pub theatres.) In the example of Alex's Tube trip above, we can see that there is potentially more than one reasonable way:

- Alex could 'reasonably' say that the trip had two purposes – one business and one pleasure. And that therefore they will divide the cost in half, and allow half.

- They could equally 'reasonably' say that the casting call took two hours and the drink with Ollie took one hour, and that therefore they will claim two-thirds of the cost of the trip.

And you may well be able to think of equally reasonable methods of apportioning that have not occurred to me. That is very much the point. There is no one law, no one accountant, and no one staff member at HMRC to tell you that this point must be approached in one, and only one way.

You will use the same principle for the Tube trip to London as you do when you consider, say, an overseas trip that has both business and personal elements. Perhaps you are on tour in Germany, but then you come back to the UK via Switzerland because you visit your cousin Georgie there on the way back. This means that your flight back from Switzerland to the UK inherently has a mixed purpose, and you will need to come up with a reasonable way of apportioning it.

Let's now consider some of the most commonly apportioned expenses for creative sole traders, and some of the most common reasonable ways I suggest of dealing with them. At risk of repetition: don't go looking for 'one-size-fits-all' here. Remember the tribunal judge who said that freelancers' working patterns were 'infinitely variable'. Consider how the principles are most reasonably applied or not, in your particular circumstances.

Mobile phone

There is, of course, a huge variety of deals and tariffs, so you need to consider this carefully and ask yourself what proportion of the expenses you incur can reasonably be allocated to business use. For many people, a ballpark percentage of 50–80% will be the right one.

Home landline and/or Wi-Fi/broadband

We will talk about 'Use of Home as Office' expenses on page 96; there are special rules about rent and utilities. But these *do not apply to telecoms at home*. For telecoms at home, apply a simple % based on the principles just discussed. Again, for many people the answer here will be 50–80%.

Professional appearance, e.g. haircuts, make-up, special beauty products or treatments, etc.

Some items are wholly for your business; for example, stage make-up and haircuts for actors. But it is reasonable to apportion, for example, ordinary make-up and beauty products, because you may well use more of these as an actor than you would in another profession.

Larger purchases, e.g. laptop, phone

Same thing – make a reasonable estimate – how many hours of your usage every day are business and how many are personal?

It is vanishingly unlikely that you would ever be asked to actually present any evidence for the figure you have chosen. But you might be asked to say why you think it is a reasonable one – so be sure about what you would say if you were asked.

Use of vehicles

We'll talk later about the special rules on this. See page 100.

iv. Use of your home as your office

Thinking about the proportion of a cost that is dedicated to professional as opposed to private life brings us on to working from home, which many creatives will be doing, and how to think about this in tax terms.

'Use of Home as Office' is tax-speak for a line which will appear in the expenditure list for all creative freelancers. Any freelancer who works from home can claim a proportion of the expenses of running their home, because they are using their home as an office.

At first glance, it might be thought that Alex doesn't do any/much work from home, but that's not really the case, and it isn't HMRC's view. When Alex is emailing engagers, or making self-tapes, or organising the diary, or the thousand-and-one other things that a freelancer has to do, they are working – and in all probability they are doing these things at home.

There is carefully worded guidance from HMRC about this matter, and paying close attention to the wording is likely to save you some money, if you are willing to do some simple calculations.

Some taxpayers have told me that they use 'a table which HMRC publish' to give a rate for this expense item. Some have even told me that their understanding is that they are *obliged* to use it.

It is true that HMRC publish a table. It is also true that you can use it if you want. It is emphatically not true that you are obliged to use it; and if you don't use it, but do the slightly more complex calculation yourself, you will probably save money.

There are three main types of expense that Alex's claim is based on:

- Rent, or interest on mortgage where you are a homeowner (remember that it's only the *interest portion* of your mortgage that's the 'expense', not the whole monthly repayment).

- Light, heat and water.

- Council Tax.

- Some people may also have insurance and cleaning costs.

Remember that, as mentioned above, phone/IT/broadband are treated entirely separately, because they are so much more fundamental to your business than the other items. So Alex does not include them here – they deal with these costs separately, as discussed in the table above. Most self-employed people working from home will claim a much higher percentage of their Wi-Fi costs than their use-of-home costs.

So, for the main three 'Use of Home as Office' costs, HMRC offers Alex the use of their simplified table. '*Simplified expenses,*' they say, helpfully, '*are a way of calculating some of your business expenses using flat rates instead of working out your actual business costs.*'

They're not saying you *have* to use this method. They're saying you can if you want.

They are also saying that because the rate is a '*flat rate*', it is a 'no-questions-asked' item: Alex can claim it without the obligation to produce receipts if asked.

Let's see it in practice.

Alex works at home more than 101 hours a month, so the simplified checker offers an allowance of £26 per month, or £312 for the year.

But now let's see Alex's workings-out the alternative, longer way, and find out if it makes a difference.

They add up their total annual rent or mortgage interest cost, total gas and electricity bills, and total Council Tax:

Rent: £12,000
Bills: £750
Council Tax: £1,000
Total: £13,750

Now Alex works out the proportion of home space they use for work, remembering storage space, and space they use for filming self-tapes, setting out equipment, etc. Most people will probably get to approximately 15% of their home space used for work purposes. Alex does not need to get a tape-measure out here. A reasonable approximation is fine.

Another way to do this is to count the number of rooms you have except kitchens and bathrooms, and claim the

% of number of rooms that you use for work. So if your house has two reception rooms, three bedrooms and an office/study, you will claim 1/6 or 17%. (Be careful if you live in a bedsit and therefore think you can claim 100% by this method. That's (obviously) not using the method in the way it is intended – it's intended to identify rooms wholly used for work in a larger property.)

Say Alex decides on 15% of space used, and works at home on average for three days per week (3/7). This gets us over the 101 hours per month. Again, Alex is not obliged to analyse the 365 days of their diary to come up with this 3/7 figure. They should just consider the year and make a reasonable estimate, based on a reasonable working year, with a reasonable amount of holiday.

We then multiply the total cost (£13,750) by the proportion of space (x 15%) by the proportion of time (x 3/7):

£13,750 x 15% x 3/7 = a claim of £884.

This is £572 more than the £312 claim Alex would make by using the simplified method. Using the longer calculation, they can save at least £115 off their tax bill, in this case.

Obviously, the higher your rent and the smaller your living space, the more beneficial the longer calculation method. Alex scores here with the long method because they share a flat in London, which means high rent for small space. Gordon, the homeowner of a mansion in rural Norfolk, who has a lot of equity in it, which means low mortgage for large space, may well be better off with the simplified £312 allowance.

v. Use of vehicles

Questions around expenses incurred while using your home as your office might naturally lead you on to think about your car, if you own one.

Most creatives do some work from their personal home, and equally they might have to transport themselves to various places in a personal car. Unless their vehicle is central to the nature of their work (e.g. taxi drivers, builders), most self-employed people tend to use their personal private vehicle both for business and personal use.

Alex does not have a car – what's the point, in Hoxton? – but Gordon, living in that Norfolk mansion, does. It would be absurd for Gordon to have two cars, one for business and one for pleasure. Of course he only has one, and uses it both to drive to the station to catch the train to London for rehearsals, and to go to the supermarket on Saturdays.

So let's look at how Gordon might think about his car in expense terms. In broad terms, tax law provides two specific ways of apportioning the expenses of the use of your private vehicle in your business:

The simple 'mileage' method

For vehicles, unlike our conclusion above re: 'Use of Home as Office', you will usually be better off with the simplified method.

Using the simple mileage method allows Gordon to claim an allowance of 45p per mile for a car (for the first 10,000 miles a year – the rate goes down when you go over that) and smaller allowances for use of a bike or motorbike.

You can check the up-to-date rates by visiting www.gov.uk and searching for 'mileage and fuel allowances'. The 45p allowance *covers every cost of the car* – fuel, insurance, repairs, and a notional contribution to the cost of the car itself.

So if Gordon uses the mileage method, he does not need to account for any of the actual costs he pays. He just needs to add up his business miles as he goes along, perhaps using an app, or a good old notebook-in-the-glovebox. The only extra costs he accounts for on top are parking and toll charges.

Thus the mileage method is much easier to administer and, in my experience, usually provides a larger deduction than the second method I'm about to outline.

The capital allowance and proportion method

As an alternative, Gordon can adopt a more complex method which involves two separate types of expense:

i. A capital allowance for the purchase price of his car.

ii. A proportion of all the running costs.

Strict and complex rules govern the amount of capital allowance that Gordon can claim each year against the initial purchase price of the car. The actual rate varies according to the type of car and various other factors, but it is often 6%. Therefore, unless he bought a very expensive car, the amount claimed is likely to be very small, in comparison to the mileage rate, especially if he has clocked up a few thousand business miles.

If Gordon uses this method, he will also need to estimate what percentage of his use of the car is for business as opposed to personal purposes. Let's say it is 25%: he will then need to calculate and claim 25% of the cost of all the fuel, repairs and other running costs.

Note, too, that Gordon is *not allowed to switch* between the mileage method and the capital allowance method from year to year with regard to the same vehicle – once he has started using one method, he must stick to the same one for the life of that vehicle.

vi. Travel when you often go to the same place

Having dealt with how to account for mileage in your own vehicle, if you have one, and if you use it to travel to different places of work, let us move on to a related question: how to define travel expenses more broadly, regardless of the method of travel used.

This is one of the most complex areas for actors and other freelance creatives to think about, because of the varied nature of their work. You definitely need to deploy the mantra of different workers having 'an infinite variety of circumstances'. Here are some rules of thumb:

- At its most basic, freelance sole traders tend to use their home as their business address, especially in the creative industries, and so there is zero cost of travel from your home to your 'usual place of business'.

- But when you travel to a rehearsal, a performance, a research trip, a dance class or a production meeting, your travel is usually allowable because you are going from one place of work (your desk at home) to another (the rehearsal room). The nature of your work is such that you are usually 'outside the normal pattern of work' – a bit like a taxi driver or a plumber, you go to all kinds of different places, rather than to the same place all the time; therefore you don't really have a 'normal pattern'; and therefore all your travel is likely to be allowable.

- Occasionally, though, you may have a period of time in what might be considered 'normal pattern'. For example:

  - You are an actor appearing in a West End show for a year.

  - You get a teaching contract with a college to teach one or two days a week for six months, always at the college.

Under these circumstances, you will have to decide what is your 'normal pattern' and what is not, in order to work out your travel expenses. Some of the factors that will influence your judgement will include:

- What you are doing in the hours that you are not working on the 'regular' gig. For example, if you are in a West End show for a year, what are you doing on non-matinee daytimes? Do you have the rest of that time off, and stay at home? Or are you always out at dance classes and auditions for films and TV? Probably a mixture between the two…

- Do you repeat the same journey very regularly – do you always travel from Tube or rail station A to the same station B? Or are your journeys more varied, and if so, why?

- How much work on the 'regular' contract is done at places other than the regular venue? For example, if you are teaching at a college, do you also do research for that work in other locations? If you are on a long show contract at one theatre, are there also, for example, schools workshops at schools that you visit on some daytimes?

Here are a couple of examples which should help shed some more light:

> Abbey is a musical theatre performer. She lives in Tooting and gets a one-year contract on *Les Mis* in the West End. On the six show-days every week, she gets the same Tube at the same time from Tooting to Leicester Square. She decides that she will not do any other work during the year; she plans to use her mornings for resting, domestic chores, and sometimes gym or dance classes. She walks to a local gym, and she usually goes to dance classes in the West End, but at different locations and different times.
>
> I tend to advise Abbey that most of her travel costs are not allowable, because she is really only working in one place and she is travelling to it in a very regular pattern. I advise allowing a very small proportion of the travel cost insofar as it relates to the dance classes. It's for Abbey to propose a reasonable basis on which to apportion those expenses.

> Ines is a writer and yoga teacher. Her working week tends to be varied. Some days she writes at home, other days in a café, other days at a hot-desking hub. She teaches yoga at a variety of locations. She has one yoga teaching gig that has lasted several years, once a week at the same time at a particular gym. She also lectures half a day per week on creative writing at a college. The schedule for this is a bit fluid; term-time teaching is about thirty-three weeks a year, and the college sometimes change the day and site of her session depending on other timetabling needs.

> I advise that there is enough flexibility and change in Ines' schedule that she is entitled to claim all her travel expenses. I feel open to a challenge from HMRC about the journeys to the longer-term yoga class. They might argue that this is so regular that the travel cost should not be allowable. But I'm inclined to fight this, because in the overall varied context of Ines' working life, I think the fact that she always goes to the same place just for one session per week is largely irrelevant.

In one sense I am sorry not to be able to give you a hard-and-fast answer to this area, which I know is a tricky one for creatives to have to work out. But the situation is that tax law simply sets out the principles we are discussing, and leaves you to make your own honest and reasonable judgement about your own particular case. Consider it as best you can, and be prepared to say why you think what you have done is reasonable, should you ever be asked to do so.

vii. Health and wellbeing

Now that we've dealt with where you live and how you move around, in expense terms, let's take a look at expenses you might incur looking after yourself, something that crops up in a variety of ways for actors in particular. This is where things get really unclear, so buckle in. I get so many questions about this area, and it's so opaque, that it's worth getting into the detail of precedents and tribunals to try to unpick it.

The general rule in tax is that *expenditure on the personal health of a sole trader is NOT a business expense.*

This may, for an actor, seem counterintuitive and unfair. After all, we have established that expenses are allowable when they are used for work, and if your health requires an expense to enable you to work, that should count, right? Isn't your body your tool for work?

Say, for example, that you are an actor who has a bad back, and that unless you have some massage, or sit in a special chair, you are simply unable to stand still or sit for longer than ten minutes without a break, and even that is painful. Obviously this will render work in the creative industries either very difficult or impossible.

Or say that you're an actor and you need reading glasses, or a hearing aid. If you can't read scripts and you can't hear what others are saying to you without spending money on the solution, it seems intuitive to describe the amounts spent on the solution as used for work.

Tax law rejects it, however, because there are two fundamental problems with this intuition:

Generality

First, the intuitive argument would apply to any human in the workforce, not just sole traders in the creative industries. Absence of back pain, the ability to read text, and the ability to hear what others are saying are as necessary to function effectively as a supermarket checkout assistant, as they are to be an actor. So if these expenses were allowable, it would follow that they would need to be allowable for everyone in the workforce. Everyone who wears glasses (which is the great majority of the population over the age of 45) would need to fill in a tax return to reclaim the cost of their eyecare. And this is not the case.

Dual use

The second difficulty is that tax law disallows expenditure which has what it calls 'an intrinsic duality of purpose', i.e. a purpose which is not only supporting your business but also your life in other respects.

In tax law's consideration of expenses for self-employment, the words 'wholly and exclusively' are there but the word 'necessarily' is not. 'Necessarily' only applies to the expenses of employment, not self-employment, as we will see later (on page 128). So in tax-law terms, you are barking up the wrong tree if you are asking yourself, 'Did I *need* to spend this money to support my business?' That's the wrong question. The right question is 'Was there a *second purpose* to the expenditure that was to do with my personal life and not my business?' And for you to claim the expense, in essence the answer has to be 'No, there was not. There was only the business purpose.'

We have already discussed above that even though the principle seems fairly clear, in practice the answers can become very complex and tangled. We have mentioned, for example, that food and drink will sometimes be allowable, even though it could hardly be more obvious that it has an 'intrinsic duality of purpose' – it is keeping you alive, as well as being necessary for your business.

But we will see in the section below that, if the expenditure could *not reasonably be avoided* because of the nature of your work – e.g. dinner out when away on tour – then it is allowable. In this case we're no longer talking about *duality*, we are talking about *causality*. Because you are working far away from home, it is exclusively because of your business that you eat somewhere that isn't your own kitchen.

This issue of what counts as a justifiable expense when it comes to looking after body and appearance, when your trade as a professional actor at some level depends on it, is a confusing matter to wrap your head around.

I think that the best approach is for us to analyse some principles established by tax tribunal precedents, then apply these to some everyday scenarios. After this you'll be in a better position to consider whether your own particular situation needs further analysis, if it does not quite fit any of the established scenarios.

> *Norman vs. Golder:*
> *Medical care is general rather than professional*
>
> In 1944 (well, there wasn't much else going on at the time, lol), Mr Norman went all the way to the Court of Appeal, one of the highest Courts in the land, to argue that he should be allowed to claim the doctors' bills he had paid to keep himself going in work as a writer after a severe illness.
>
> Unfortunately for him, Lord Greene, the most senior lawyer in the UK at the time, disagreed, saying:
>
> 'Expenses of that kind are not wholly and exclusively laid out for the purposes of the trade, profession or vocation; they are laid out in part for *advantage as a living human being.*'
>
> HMRC's manual adds an additional sentence which helps us navigate the tricky boundary here: 'There will almost always be a *personal purpose in wishing to enjoy better health.*'
>
> This is a helpful sentence, for two key reasons. One, it follows that if there is no personal purpose, then the

> expenditure is more likely to be allowable. Two, it tells us that, if the motivation for the expenditure is something *other* than 'wishing to enjoy better health', then we do not apply the precedent of Norman vs. Golder.

Let's pick up the example of Alex and their eyesight, which we mentioned much earlier in this chapter, when we were discussing surprisingly allowable expenses (on page 90). Now (and I'm sure you've been waiting with bated breath) we can deconstruct our surprise, and see that it's reasonable for Alex to claim for contact lenses.

Alex, who is short-sighted, spends money on getting contact lenses instead of glasses. They do this because their agent has advised them that it is better to have complete consistency of appearance between how they appear in headshots and showreels, and how they appear in person. Alex rather dislikes the feel of contact lenses, and the hassle of the daily maintenance. They wouldn't have chosen to make this purchase but for their agent's advice.

Now Alex has reasonable grounds to claim the expense because, even though it could be said that the contact lenses work to their 'advantage as a human being', Alex did not lay out the expenditure for the 'personal purpose in wishing to enjoy better health'. They did it for purely professional reasons – and indeed somewhat against their personal wishes.

Prince vs. Mapp:
Medical care specifically incurred to ply one's trade

In 1969, Mr Prince paid for an operation to fix the little finger of his left hand after he had injured it sharpening a pencil. He claimed the expense of the surgery on his tax return. Mr Mapp disagreed with this deduction, and off they went to tribunal.

Incidentally… in case you are wondering who Mr Golder and Mr Mapp were – they were tax inspectors. It used to be a wonderful quirk of tax tribunals that the tax inspector who was processing the file in question was put up in person, in court, as the face of the State. Nowadays this cute quirk has been lost – if Alex takes a case to tribunal today, it will go on the record as Alex Actor vs. plain old HMRC. I do wonder what Mr Golder and Mr Mapp were really like in person, though. I mention their names almost every day and I'd have liked to have had a beer with them.

Why did Mr Prince pay to get his finger fixed? Well, his day job was as an architect, but he also played guitar in a band, and the band was good enough to get paid for this, playing at functions, in pubs, etc. Mr Prince argued that he needed to pay for the operation in order to continue playing the guitar. The judge, Mr Justice Pennycuick, agreed with him:

'Someone carrying on a trade or profession incurs some injury which is trivial in itself and *in respect of which he would never otherwise expend money on medical care but which happens to be of vital importance for the purpose of that particular trade or profession*. In such a case I am prepared to assume in favour of the taxpayer here, that it would be possible for a taxpayer to incur expense which was wholly and exclusively for the purpose of his trade or profession.'

Note the words I have italicised. If you are considering whether or not to claim expenses of this kind, it is vital that you ask yourself whether or not you would have chosen to spend the money were it not for the needs of your particular business – and the answer will vary from person to person and from time to time.

Side note – Mr Prince actually lost his case in the end, because he was asked if he also played the guitar as a hobby, for his personal pleasure, as well as for his gigging work. He said yes, and so Mr Justice Pennycuick ruled against him, despite his comments quoted above. If Mr Prince was playing the guitar as a hobby, then it followed that the operation had helped his hobby as well as his gigging work. A hobby is a personal pursuit, not a trade pursuit, and therefore Mr Prince's claim was disallowed.

A very tricky area.

Osborne vs. HMRC:
Gym expenses

Let's get to grips with what we've all been waiting for – gym membership expenses for performers and musicians. Here, a more recent tribunal case will help us, brought in 2020 by Mr Osborne, a deep-sea diver...

I have asked many groups of drama school students to judge based on their intuition whether an actor ought to be allowed to deduct gym expenses or not. The great majority tend to judge that they ought to. Intuitively we tend to think that an actor's body is their 'toolkit', as it were, and therefore that the cost of keeping it fit and healthy should be deductible, in the same way that a mechanic could certainly claim for the cost of cleaning and oiling their spanners.

However, given our discussion above, we can perhaps now see that there is a problem here. It would be hard to argue that the expense of going to the gym is not 'laid out in part for advantage as a living human being'. The general principle of Norman vs. Golder appears to suggest that going to the gym is not allowable. This is because in almost every imaginable profession, a case could be made that increased physical fitness will result in increased performance. Even in my own trade, slave to my monitor and keyboard though I am, I have discovered that an hour in the gym at lunchtime often makes me more alert and more focused in the afternoon, knocking out tax returns quicker and much more effectively than if I had gone to the pub for an hour instead.

So let's now draw together three important perspectives and see if we can apply them to develop our analysis:

- **Specificity**: everyone's work is slightly different to everyone else's – the correct answer in tax for Alex may not be the same as the correct answer for Jo, even if they are both performers.

- **Professional not personal**: '*would never otherwise expend… but… happens to be of vital importance to that particular trade*' – we remember Mr Justice Pennycuick's introduction of the concept of a person's motivation to spend the money, and what they would choose to do if they were in another profession.

- **Appearance as professional matter of importance to actors**: the distinction, especially for actors, between expenditure on *health* (clinical, linked to function, general) and expenditure on *appearance* (cosmetic, linked to decoration, specific) – because appearance is of particular importance to the market actors have to operate in, for obvious reasons.

With these three matters in mind, let's look at the case of Mr Osborne.

> …Mr Osborne is a deep-sea diver who claimed his gym expenses. HMRC sent him a recalculation notice disallowing these, relying on that key judgement of Norman vs. Golder and the obvious fact that attending a gym will improve anyone's health at a personal level.
>
> Mr Osborne objected to the recalculation. HMRC dug their heels in, so Mr Osborne went to first-tier tribunal, representing himself without an accountant or solicitor – brave man!
>
> Mr Osborne gave detailed evidence to the effect that he spent a lot of time in the gym – much more than a casual or 'normal' gym-user would, and that he did a lot of exercises specifically designed to work on his breathing (obviously relevant to his profession). He supplied detailed information from his professional body describing exactly what breathing capabilities are necessary or useful for divers. And he stated that, self-evidently, he would not have spent so much time doing these things had he not needed to do so for his work.
>
> This was enough for Judge Nicholl to agree with him and to allow his claim.

There has never been a tribunal case considering the same matter in relation to actors, dancers or musical theatre performers. So this is not a point on which you can rely to the same degree of confidence that you could if you were a deep-sea diver. That said, you will clearly be able to see how some of these points are likely to be transferrable to someone working, or trying to get work, in areas such as dance, physical theatre or musical theatre, because these people are likely to:

- Spend more time in the gym than is normal for most people.

- Do exercises in the gym that they learned during their professional training and that are specifically designed to enhance professional capability.

- Feel that they would not do either of these things but for their trade.

> *Parsons vs. HMRC*
>
> In another tribunal case, brought by Mr Parsons, a stunt performer, who also represented himself at tribunal in 2010, gym expenses were disallowed. I consider that Mr Parsons was not specific enough about the three points above to succeed in his claim.

Another situation we come across often is where actors have been told, either by agents or casting directors when going up for a role, or by producers once they have been cast, to adjust their body shape in preparation for a role. This still happens not infrequently, especially in film and TV, whatever we may think of the cultural politics of such an instruction; and it happens more frequently when the actors concerned are required to appear without clothes in the role. Such an instruction to an actor is more likely to help the actor claim that the expense can be deducted, since there is a direct relationship between their decision to go to the gym and the instruction or preference of their engager.

So the conclusion is not simple, and not applicable to everyone; but I hope this analysis helps you decide where you personally stand in relation to this point.

Physiotherapy, psychotherapy, and related treatments

Now that we have dealt with gym membership, a related area in which similar questions come up frequently for performers is in relation to the cost of treatments such as physiotherapy or osteopathy. Perhaps Alex will benefit from such treatments, or from massage, and perhaps these are helping to fix or improve a problem that was itself caused by work.

Similar questions are also sometimes asked about psychotherapy and counselling: it could be said that an actor or writer might improve their public-facing work if psychotherapy gives them better insight into their own emotions, in a sense comparable to the sense in which I might improve my tap skills by going to a tap class. Or perhaps an actor has experienced trauma when rehearsing and performing material that they have found distressing, and needs a talking treatment to heal.

By now you know the first things I'm going to say about this, don't you?

Right. There's no hard-and-fast rule, it depends on each person's scenario, and you need to think about the case law (especially, with this question, Norman vs. Golder and Prince vs. Mapp) and think about what applies to you.

First, there is no tribunal case at which an actor's or writer's or director's claim to such treatments has been directly tested in law; although more helpfully Mr Parsons, the stunt specialist, won his claim for chiropractor and massage expenses at his 2010 tribunal. The judge repeated the standard disclaimer about every case being different – '[this] will always be a question that is case-specific' – and said helpfully, quoting an earlier precedent, that what mattered in this case was '*the special character* [*of the treatments*] *dictated by the occupation as a matter of physical necessity*'.

Second, all the historical cases tell us that it doesn't matter how an injury was sustained in the first place: what matters is its effect on work versus its effect on other aspects of a person's life. Mr Norman said that his condition had worsened because of what he was doing at work, but that didn't help him win his case; Mr Prince fully agreed that he'd cut his finger at his day job, not while gigging, and that did no harm to his argument that it affected his gigging. He lost his case because playing guitar was his hobby as well as providing an income stream.

Therefore Alex's claim for osteopathy to help them with some back trouble is not affected by the question of whether the trouble was caused or exacerbated by dancing. It is affected by whether Alex will or won't be able to work in future unless they pay for the cost of an osteopath or physio, and how special or specific is the nature of the treatment.

I find Mr Justice Pennycuick's comments in Prince vs. Mapp useful here: '[*The taxpayer*] *incurs some injury which is trivial in itself and in respect of which he would never otherwise expend money on medical care but which happens to be of vital importance for the purpose of that particular trade or profession.*'

I think there are two useful benchmarks in this sentence:

- **The relative triviality of an injury.** We all know a friend or family member who works in an office job and harbours the vague intention to get some physio to sort out their mild back pain at some point, but we also know that many of these never quite get round to it, because the problem is relatively trivial. Alex is much more likely to pay for physio themselves, because of its 'vital importance for the purpose of their profession'.

- **The relationship between the nature of the injury and the type of work.** It is obvious to anyone involved in the performing arts that physiotherapy, osteopathy, etc. are used very commonly in certain types of work. Touring theatre and dance companies will often research and maintain lists of physiotherapists in the towns they are visiting. It is common for a dancer to come off stage in the evening and ask the company manager to book them a physio appointment for the next day, and in many cases the company will pay for it. This does not happen to teachers, architects or traffic wardens. It also happens less commonly in 'straight' (non-physical) theatre than in physical theatre or dance; but perhaps a straight play has a fight scene, for example, which requires the participants to do unusual and precise moves. It all depends on the circumstances.

Consider that a professional football team is bound to employ a massage therapist – several of these, full time, in the case of Premier League clubs. They are doing this because it is a normal part of football and obviously not a part of most other professions. It would be nonsense to suggest that the clubs should not be allowed to deduct the cost of these massages from their profits. And so I argue that the more normal the cost of a treatment is for your particular profession or activity, the stronger your claim to deduct it. Remember the comment of the judge in the Parsons case: they allowed expenses concerning '*the special character* [*of the treatments*] *dictated by the occupation as a matter of physical necessity*'.

I find it very hard, however, to make the same argument in relation to psychotherapy or counselling. It seems to me that pretty much by definition these are not 'trivial' investigations. Psychotherapists and their clients are likely to discuss profound, life-changing matters, of major import to the person, but not necessarily to the purpose of a particular trade or profession. So that tends to suggest to me that it is pretty much impossible for actors or writers to deduct those kinds of costs.

Expenses connected to disability

Much the same consideration applies to the question of whether a freelancer with a disability can claim expenses which assist them to work.

Here are some common examples:

- The cost of treatments or medical procedures that assist you: apply the same principles discussed above, especially with reference to the Prince vs. Mapp and Parsons cases.

- More expensive travel costs than would be the case for a non-disabled person; for example, because you need to take a taxi for a trip which a non-disabled person would usually make by Tube: this will be wholly allowable. It doesn't matter how much an expense costs – what matters is whether the expense was incurred wholly for work.

- The cost of specialist software that assists you – consider whether the software is used only for work, or a mixture of work and other uses. If the former, it is wholly claimable; if the latter, you need to estimate a reasonable proportion to claim.

The Department for Work and Pensions' Access to Work scheme (explained at gov.uk/access-to-work) funds many of these kinds of costs, and others. It can be a tricky scheme to navigate, but if you are eligible and succeed in an application, then the question of whether or not expenses can be allowed for tax becomes irrelevant, because they are funded by a grant, and therefore there is no expense to you at the end of the day. For the purposes of your tax return, you simply ignore money received from the DWP for Access to Work, and your spending of that money on the expenses concerned, when you fill in your return.

viii. Clothes and personal appearance

This section is relevant almost exclusively to performers. For others, no costs connected to professional appearance or clothing will usually be allowable, except that items of clothing very specifically used for work and only for work, i.e. a kind of uniform, may be allowable. For example, if a lighting designer buys a pair of steel-toecapped working boots and only ever uses these when working on stage during tech work, then these will be allowable.

Actors and dancers, for obvious reasons, will incur expenses whose entire purpose is to create or maintain their physical appearance in a certain way. Some items that support this are evidently wholly for your business; for example, stage make-up and haircuts. It is also reasonable to apportion, for example, ordinary make-up and beauty products, because you may well use more of these as an actor than you would in another profession.

Clothing is a much trickier and more restricted area. Only two types of clothing are allowable without any doubt:

- Clothes that are very particular in type and can only be used for that purpose; for example, tap shoes or ballet shoes.

- Clothes that you buy to wear onstage or on screen – costumes, in effect. Mostly, of course, the producer of a piece will provide your costume; but in some kinds of everyday work such as short film, roleplay, etc., you will often be asked to provide your own costume, and this will then be allowable. It is viewed as similar in tax law to a traffic warden's uniform, or an undertaker's top hat – it is a specific item expressly required by an engager or employer in those particular circumstances.

I am often asked about allowing items of clothing which were 'bought for work' but which do not fall into either of these categories. Some common examples:

- You are filming a self-tape for an ad for a new product which is to be marketed to young adults. You judge that you are more likely to be cast if you wear a Stone Island T-shirt, so you go out and buy one. Had it not been for that particular self-tape, you would not have bought the T-shirt.

- You are nominated for a BAFTA. Obviously you have to look good for the ceremony, and you don't have a suitable suit, dress, etc., because the one you wore for cousin Kevin's wedding three years ago doesn't fit, so you go out and buy one – which you would not have done were it not for the ceremony.

- You prefer to rehearse in loose-fitting tracksuit bottoms and you never wear them for any other purpose.

These expenses are almost certainly *not* claimable, which (sorry, I know it's confusing) runs counter to the principle we took great trouble to establish above, about the extent to which expenses would not have been incurred 'but for' your work. The problem with clothing is caused by a particular 1983 tribunal case:

> *Mallalieu vs. Drummond*
>
> Ms (later Baroness – arguing with HMRC at tribunal won't necessarily stop you rising to the pinnacle of British society) Mallalieu was a barrister. She claimed not only the cost of her wigs and gowns (evidently allowable like 'uniform' or 'costume'), but also the cost of her business suits for travelling to and from court, meeting clients, colleagues and solicitors in her chambers, etc.
>
> Her argument was that she didn't like wearing suits and only did so because it was expected by clients and solicitors in the course of her work. She could hardly turn up to such meetings in jeans or swimsuits, which would not give her professional credibility.
>
> But the courts rejected her argument. In the Court of Appeal, Lord Brightman said that 'there is an inevitable private purpose in acquiring normal civilian clothing even when it is only used for the purposes of the trade, profession or vocation'. We can infer from this that if the item of clothing concerned is a 'normal civilian' item then it will not be allowable, even if it was only bought with work in mind.

We can see that this cuts out the Stone Island T-shirt and the jogging bottoms worn at rehearsal, because there is an 'inevitable private purpose' in these 'normal civilian' pieces of clothing.

It probably disallows the outfit for the BAFTA ceremony too. Why only 'probably'? Well, I think we need to allow room for the fact that sometimes performers appear offstage – on the red carpet at the BAFTAs, say – dressed in items which you would not describe as 'normal civilian' clothing. Thus the more strange or idiosyncratic the outfit, the more you might be tempted to back a claim for it, and vice versa.

One more tribunal case to mention in passing, which shows how finely balanced this point is:

> In 2018, Gemma Daniels, a dancer at Stringfellows adult nightclub, went to tribunal after HMRC tried to disallow the cost of the dresses, lingerie and shoes that she bought and wore in her act. These are 'normal civilian' clothes, right? So you can see how HMRC argued that that should be disallowed. But Ms Daniels won that part of her case, the judges agreeing with her that this expenditure was 'akin to the acquisition of a costume by a self-employed actor for use in a performance', even though the clothes themselves were standard, off-the-shelf items. What swung it for her was her insistence that they were a costume for a show, in her case.

Cosmetic procedures

HMRC's manual states that slightly different considerations apply to medical or quasi-medical expenses that are designed to make cosmetic improvements to a performer's appearance. This is a very difficult area because, as we have seen above, an important consideration is the 'counterfactual' – the decision about spending on their appearance that a person might have taken if they were not a performer, and the extent to which they would not have incurred the expenditure but for the needs of their profession.

HMRC's internal guidance argues that only in exceptional circumstances would a person have no private motive for '*reversing or masking the advancing of the years*' (how quaint their phraseology!), and they clearly hope that performers will be reticent about making claims to allow these kinds of expenses.

But there are several reasons why some performers might, in some circumstances, nevertheless feel that a claim is justifiable:

- Many types of cosmetic procedure are unpleasant and uncomfortable to experience, and so it seems to me that a performer may well decide to undertake it *expressly and only* for the professional motive.

- Sometimes performers are told or advised by agents, casting directors, producers or directors to undertake procedures, which seems to me to make their private motivation rather less relevant.

It is very difficult to give conclusive advice about this, because this particular point has not been tested often enough at tribunal, although Mr Parsons the stunt man did succeed in arguing for this deduction in relation to cosmetic dentistry. If you are concerned about it, you will have to think carefully about all the issues raised above and make the decision for yourself that you feel is most fair and reasonable.

Remember that if you decide to claim an expense to which HMRC should ever object, you will have to explain, perhaps robustly, why you believe it is a reasonable one, and you will need to do so in the terms and according to the arguments that I have set out above. If you lose the argument, you will have to pay any tax due on the expense that you claimed (probably at the rate of either 20% or 40% of it) and you may have to pay interest and penalties as well. So don't take this fight on without considering the strength of your particular case carefully, and consider discussing it with a specialist accountant.

x. Subsistence and accommodation

We saw above (on page 91) that reasonable expenses for the normal costs of living such as accommodation, food and drink are often likely to be allowable when you are working away from home, and I gave you some basic rules of thumb to help you judge whether a particular meal may or may not be allowable.

There is one last tribunal case very important to our field which I would like to discuss because it sheds some more light on these matters: a case concerning the actor Tim Healy in 2012–14. Tim is an actor who will be familiar to many older people because of his roles in, among other popular shows, *Auf Wiedersehen Pet* and *Benidorm*.

Healy vs. HMRC

In 2005–06 Tim, who lived near Manchester, spent a year in the West End appearing in the musical *Billy Elliot*. Rather than stay in a hotel for the length of the assignment, he decided to rent a flat in London for the whole period. He claimed to deduct the cost of the rent of the flat and a certain amount of subsistence. HMRC objected, and a two-year tribunal with three separate hearings was the fun result.

Tim lost his case. Because he is quite a well-known actor, there was some publicity about the case at the time. An unfortunate consequence of this is that some accountants, who remember the fact that Tim lost but do not understand very much about the details, interpret the fact that he lost to infer that 'actors are not allowed to deduct accommodation and subsistence costs'. In fact, the truth is generally the reverse; there were very specific reasons why Tim lost his case that will not apply to most creative freelancers staying away from home. The judgements of the three hearings were very useful to us, in that they illuminated some of the reasons why this is so.

First, in relation to accommodation, the principle was established that there is no reason why someone doing a job away from home for some months should not rent a property and have that expense deducted, in the same way as if it were a bill for a hotel room. Unfortunately Tim lost his case on this point, because he stated that he had rented a flat with several bedrooms so that he could host family and friends for visits to London. This fact was held by the tribunal to create a personal, rather than a professional expense. It follows pretty clearly that if Tim had instead decided to rent a studio flat, then the tribunal would have agreed that the expense could be deducted.

Second, in relation to subsistence, the tribunal told us three useful things:

i. That in general terms, if expenditure on subsistence is 'incidental' to expenditure on allowable

> accommodation, then it will usually be allowable; for example, if the accommodation is in a hotel.
>
> ii. However, that expenditure on subsistence 'in a flat' is not incidental to the accommodation in the same way that a meal in a hotel is incidental to the stay in the hotel room.
>
> iii. That it is *critical to keep receipts for subsistence*. The judges said in effect that some of Tim's subsistence would almost certainly have been allowable if HMRC had been shown receipts for them but, unfortunately, these could not be produced.

My opinion is that the judges in the Tim Healy case have helped us be very clear on these narrow questions. But they still do not really help us with some common, related scenarios.

For example, say Alex is on tour and stays in a hotel for five nights. The Healy judgement tells us a) that if they eat in the hotel restaurant, the meal is allowable, and b) if Alex had decided to rent a flat for the week and get in a Tesco order for the week then the Tesco shop would not be allowable.

You notice that the judgement has not told us about other common situations; for example, Alex staying in the hotel but deciding to go to Tesco and buy sandwiches, fruit, TV dinners (there's a microwave in the room) and doughnuts. This seems to fall halfway between the two principles established. In the majority of cases I would tend to advise that such expenses would be allowable. To my mind, it's the fact that Alex is staying in a hotel and not a flat that is important here, not the fact that the meal came out of a packet and not out of the hotel kitchen. But my opinion about this has not been tested at a tribunal.

Bearing in mind the words of the judge in the older case which I quoted earlier – 'the facts of such cases are infinitely variable' – what principles can we rely on that will be applicable to most absences from home, say for performers on tour, or writers away on research trips?

As always, everything will ultimately turn on you and your personal circumstances, but here are some useful rules of thumb.

- If you stay away from home for work, the cost of your *accommodation* is usually allowable.

- So is the accompanying *food and drink*; unless –

- – you are away for quite a long period and rent a 'home', in which case you cannot deduct the cost of (say) a weekly supermarket shop for your rented home.

- You must *get and keep receipts for food and drink* and you must *keep them for six years* after the end of the tax year concerned.

And now one or two last odds-and-ends re. expenses for your tax return…

Pension costs

We will discuss in the next chapter that pension contributions are in general a very good thing for you to consider. Tax relief is part of the reason for this, and we'll also go into this in more detail.

But if you contribute to a personal pension or SIPP (Self-Invested Personal Pension), your contribution is not an allowable expense and should not be included in your expenses in the same way that travel and stationery should.

Charitable donations and Gift Aid

Charitable donations are also not an allowable expense for a sole trader. If you earn more than £50,000 profit in the year, and if your donation was Gift-Aided, then it is entered into a separate section of the tax return and 20% of the value is refunded to you through your tax calculation; that's to say, you are given the sweetener of being allowed to make the donation from your 20% bracket, not your 40% bracket. The charity can also claim back the basic rate tax that you pay. So, if you are a higher-rate taxpayer, Gift Aid is a great scheme because it means that when you give £1, it only actually costs you 80p but the charity gets £1.25. But do not include this in your list of allowable expenses. There is no tax relief for basic-rate taxpayers on Gift Aid donations (but the charity still claim that 25p in the pound, so Gift Aid is still a great thing to do whoever you are).

Expenses if you are on a PAYE contract

As we noted in the last chapter, the majority of creative industry engagements are freelance engagements. Sometimes, however, you may undertake work on a PAYE contract. This usually happens either because the engagement is a very long one; for example, you are a full-time permanent member of an orchestra, or you are a technician permanently based at one theatre; or because the engager is a large organisation with a policy of not engaging any sole traders. This often happens in relation to universities; for example, you are asked to do a small amount of teaching but you find that the university insists on putting you on the payroll. Or you may be performing and/or teaching children for a summer season at a holiday camp, and this may also be PAYE work.

In broad terms, these kinds of arrangements are not a problem for you. You will pay almost identical levels of tax and NIC on the amounts you earn. However, expenses are treated very differently and rather more harshly for PAYE employees than for freelancers, so it is comparatively difficult to claim expenses in the way that we have been discussing in this chapter so far.

The issue stems from the fact that the law adds an extra word to the requirement that expenses should be 'wholly and exclusively' for work, when we are talking about PAYE work: here, the expenses also have to be 'necessary'. It is not enough for you to show that you incurred the expense *only* for your work, on a PAYE contract – now you have to show that the work *could not have been done without it*.

A benchmark tribunal case from 1983 illuminated this:

> *Higginbottom vs. HMRC*
>
> The splendidly named Reverend Higginbottom claimed a deduction for the cost of a slide projector which he used during sermons at the church where he was employed as rector. HMRC disallowed this, and the tribunal agreed with them. It didn't matter that Rev Higginbottom only used the projector for the sermons and not for any personal purpose; nor that if Rev Higginbottom had been *freelance*, the same expenditure would have been allowable. The case turned on the point that it is not *necessary* to use a slide projector to give a sermon.
>
> The assumption that the law is working on here is that a PAYE employer should provide you with the necessary tools to do the job, and so there shouldn't be any need for you to claim the cost of them. This doesn't always work very fairly – Rev Higginbottom's result feels intuitively unfair to me – but there you go.

The question of travel is also treated entirely differently in relation to PAYE contracts. At least here, the principle is simple. Travel from home to your normal place of work is not allowable, end of story. If it was allowable, then everyone working in every office, shop and school would be allowed to fill in a tax return and claim a tax rebate at the end of the year, which they cannot do.

IR35

We mentioned briefly earlier that there have in the past few years been some high-profile cases involving celebrity presenters in both media and sport, such as Lorraine Kelly, Gary Lineker and Adrian Chiles. These cases are to do with a type of employment legislation called 'IR35' and usually hinge on whether contracts that were undertaken as self-employment should properly have been undertaken as employment. This is an exceptionally complex and fast-developing area of tax law, but it is very unlikely that it will concern you or that you need to pay any attention to it. It will be relevant only to contracts worth a very large fee and if you are in that position, you should in any event be signing up for specialist advice.

You can find me online really easily. ;)

Golden rules for expenses

- Read the text in this chapter about each item carefully.

- Remember that there is no hard-and-fast rule that applies to everyone.

- Keep receipts for six years.
- You can make whatever argument you like that a particular expense is reasonable and is deducted, so long as you stick to the guidelines given here. You simply need to be sure that you are making the argument with good reasons and in good faith.

5. Pensions, Mortgages, Savings, Insurance and Benefits

In this chapter, we'll leave the raw mechanics of tax and consider some other financial matters of common interest and concern. Every aspect of financial self-management is bound up in some way with taxation, and as I've got your attention for the purposes of filling out your income and expenses on your tax return correctly, we might as well have a conversation about financial matters that may seem very far off in the future, but which tend to come up as we live longer, buy more things, and are more worried about what might happen to those things – and ourselves, when we really don't want to get out of bed for the day job any more.

Pensions

What are the pros and cons of pension saving?

When older people say that they are 'in receipt of a pension', they might mean any combination of three things. It is possible to receive either one, two or three of these things, and the more of them you receive, the better:

- **The British State Pension.** This is a statutory benefit which the British government pays to everyone who has reached retirement age, an age that is fixed for everyone but which varies according to when you were born. At the time of writing, it is 67 or 68 for most people, but the trend is for it to become older. The State Pension is not means-tested but is paid to everyone who worked in the UK for at least ten years during their working life, regardless of citizenship or current country of residence.

- **A personal pension, often also called a PPP (Private Pension Plan) or sometimes a SIPP (Self-Invested Private Pension).** This is just like a personal savings account that anyone can set up for themselves but, as we will see, it is different to (say) a normal savings account because it is designated formally as a pension saving: it's intended for use in later life, unlike a building society savings account that you can dip into whenever you want to in your life. You can't just withdraw money from a PPP or a SIPP when you want to – not even in an emergency.

- **An occupational or 'employer' pension,** which is a fund into which an employer (and usually you yourself too) has paid as part of the package you get in exchange for your work. Some larger employers, like the NHS, the armed forces and the teaching and higher education professions also have medical pensions, which means amounts that you might be paid by agreement with that employer because you had to take early medical retirement from the job.

Let's consider each type of pension in turn and work out how Alex can take best advantage of them, and what choices they have in relation to these.

What is the State Pension?

We discussed in earlier chapters how everyone qualifies for the full State Pension (which at the time of writing pays around £1,000 per month to recipients). How does everyone qualify? By making between ten and thirty-five Full Years of National Insurance contributions over the course of their working lives.

Alex, like everyone, begins to have an entitlement to a State Pension after clocking up ten years of making NI contributions either through PAYE work or through their tax return. If they only clocked up ten years, though, their entitlement would amount to only around £300 per month.

For each additional year between eleven and thirty-five years, they are acquiring the right to about £25 per month more, until eventually they reach thirty-five years and qualify for the full £1,000 per month.

Past that point – say Alex reaches their thirty-five years at the age of 60, but cannot start drawing the State Pension until aged 68 – Alex would only continue to contribute to NI if they were obliged to do so because of earning more than the threshold in that year (see page 48). There would be no point in Alex contributing voluntarily past that point, while there certainly would be if they had not yet reached thirty-five years, as we discussed in Chapter 3 (on page 49).

Clocking up Full Years of NI in order to qualify for the State Pension is an absolute must for everyone. You must make sure that you are doing this correctly. You can see from the figures above that for a cost of about £200 in any one year, Alex acquires the right to receive about £300 in every year of retirement: if they live to the age of 80, they will get at least £3,000 for every £200 they contribute.

So the only possible circumstance in which it would not be a good idea to ensure that they are contributing every year, would be in the awful event that Alex is going to die before completing one full year of retirement. Otherwise, the State Pension is an automatic savings plan on offer to everyone at wonderful odds.

As described in Chapter 3 (on page 48), you should be paying your NI automatically and clocking up those Full Years as you go along. If you are in PAYE work this happens automatically; if you are self-employed you take care of it as part of your tax return, and you can always check your record in your Government Gateway account.

Let's look at the issue of retirement age in a little more detail. Alex's friend Gordon has reached the magic retirement age (say 67 in his case – the exact age changes depending on the year that you were born in) and considers whether to begin to draw his £12,000 per year. At this point, the State makes him an offer (the DWP automatically sends him a letter in the post). They say that every year Gordon wants to *delay* drawing his pension, even though he is now entitled to it, they will slightly increase what he receives in the future, once he does start drawing it.

If Gordon wants to finish or greatly reduce working, or if he is unfortunately in poor health, then he is less likely to be interested in this offer than if he intends not to reduce his work commitments just yet, and if he is in good health.

In these happy circumstances, Gordon may well be attracted by the idea of leaving it a while, continuing as he is for now, and securing a higher State Pension in the future when he decides the time has come to draw it.

Gordon is likely to have in mind the fact that the State Pension is taxable income.

Back we go to our tax basics.

The maximum £12,000 per year pension is just under the personal allowance threshold (see page 51), so if it is the only income someone receives, they will not pay tax on it.

But if Gordon has already used his personal allowance through self-employment, or intends to do so, through continuing his work as an actor, then the £12,000 pension will all be taxed. If this happens, the pension for that year will only be worth £10,000 or £7,000, net of tax (depending on how much Gordon earns from work).

So it makes financial sense to consider quite carefully whether to start the State Pension just because you reach official 'retirement age' (whatever that age is by the time you get there).

Personal pensions

Anyone working in the UK is entitled to open a personal pension plan and to contribute at least the same amount as they earn in any year, up to a large annual and lifetime limit, which you are highly unlikely to want to exceed.

It is very easy to source and open a personal pension by yourself. You will probably be familiar with household names that run them such as (these are examples, not recommendations!) Black Horse, Legal & General, Virgin Money and many others. They can all be found online or via the comparison websites. They all charge you to look after your money, but mostly very modest amounts.

Advantages

There are three main advantages to opening a personal pension.

i. **Making a better life for yourself as a pensioner.** It's hard to generalise about this, but many older people struggle to manage on the State Pension alone, especially if you have ambitions in your retirement to travel or to follow leisure pursuits. You will in all likelihood need some additional income, and saving it when you are younger is an obvious part of the solution.

ii. **Long-term savings create spending power for you which is higher later rather than earlier.** If Alex saves £100 in 2026, then it will be worth about £250 in 2076, adjusting for inflation and assuming prudent interest rates. So young Alex could spend that money on a budget return flight to Dublin now, but they'll be able to take the grandchildren too in 2076 if they save the money in a pension instead, all for the same amount of money.

iii. **It's tax-free at the point of saving.** If Alex puts money into a building society account, or any other type of investment *except* a pension, they pay that money in *after* it has been taxed; but if they pay it into a pension, they pay it in *before* it has been taxed.

> For example, it straightforwardly costs Alex £100 to put £100 into their building society account. But if Alex puts the same £100 into their personal pension, HMRC puts the tax that Alex paid on the £100 before they put it into the pension… straight back into the pension. So when Alex next looks at their pension fund statement

they will see that £125 was credited, even though they only transferred £100.

If Alex is a higher-rate taxpayer, they also get a tax rebate of the difference between higher-rate and basic-rate tax. They enter all these figures on their tax return and a credit of £20 is given against the £100 contribution. So you can see, putting items ii) and iii) together, that it actually only cost Alex £80 in 2026 to put £275 into their pocket in 2076.

Disadvantages

This analysis isn't the whole picture, unfortunately – if it were, pension contributions would, of course, be a total no-brainer. Here are some of the obvious problems and pitfalls.

- **The main disadvantage of pension saving is that it is locked away until you reach the age of 57 (from 2028 – it used to be 55).** You simply cannot take it before that – not to buy a house, not to decide that actually you'd like your Caribbean cruise now rather than in 2075, and not to pay off your mortgage or other debts. In that sense, pension saving is the least flexible type of saving.

- **Just because it's a good idea to make long-term savings for your old age, it doesn't follow that a personal pension plan is always the best way to do it.** The outcome of any investment depends on the skill of the people managing it, the choices of the people managing it, and (although fund managers hate admitting this) on good luck, too.

  It's all very well (and might be quite true) to say that the average performance of a particular pension fund is, say, 7% over your working life. And you might feel relatively pleased with that. But some funds do not perform that well, and in some cases it may be no exaggeration to say that if you had simply kept the money in the bank, maintaining your flexibility to make other investments or to spend it on the other needs of your life, you would have done just as well or even better. This depends a good deal on the choices that pension fund managers make about risk. The Equity Pension Scheme for example, which we discuss more below (on page 142), is easy for you to join, but might not necessarily make the best return compared to other funds.

If you know you could have received, say, 10% from a particular unit trust, or 15-20% from investing the same money in property over the same period, then many pension investments don't look so good. If you increase your risk, you might well increase your returns, especially if you are young and therefore have a lot of time to play this game.

And so you may decide to put a lot more effort and attention into this matter, to inform yourself much more closely about different investment strategies and, with a lot of well-informed judgement and a healthy dose of luck, you might then end up much better off.

- **Just because your contribution is tax-free when you make it, it doesn't follow that it won't be taxed when you take it out.** As we have noted above, your pension income when you take it is taxable. The State Pension is pretty much swallowing up your entire personal allowance. So if you are earning from other sources, such as a personal pension, or still doing bits and bobs of paid work in your 70s while drawing your State Pension, then it is likely that the personal pension income that you take will ultimately be taxed then, even though it wasn't when you contributed it decades earlier.

> We saw an example in the box on page 139 where in effect it had only cost Alex £80 in 2026 to receive £275 in 2076.
>
> But if Alex is taxed at basic rate in 2076 because their income is high enough – and you can be sure that Alex hopes it will be – they will only receive £220 of the £275.

That said, there are two reasons why the tax position works in favour of pension saving, even if you do end up paying some income tax on your pension when you ultimately draw it.

First, you are allowed to sugar the pill when you *first* access your pension by taking a chunk of it tax-free as a lump sum.

Second, if you are earning well in the years that you contribute, and are a higher-rate taxpayer, then you are saving tax at 40% which when you come to pay it, as a less high-earning pensioner, is more likely to be at 20% – so you make a 20% saving.

Employer pensions

Employer pensions are pretty much the same beast as personal pensions, except that you do not set them up yourself. An employer or engager sets them up and invites you to join in certain circumstances. 'Employer pensions' means all pensions created and offered by those you work for, even if they are not technically your PAYE 'employer'.

Alex, in a way very typical for a creative freelancer, comes across three examples of employer pensions in their first two years of work:

i. Alex's job on the tour of *Sleeping Beauty* was offered under an Equity contract. This means that one of the contract terms was that Alex had the right to receive contributions from the producer to the Equity Pension Scheme, a scheme to which many actors belong. A similar scheme exists for musicians, under the auspices of the Musicians' Union. These two pension schemes are run under the umbrella of Aviva, the large household-name pensions and insurance company.

ii. Lauren's shop has an employer pension scheme run by The People's Pension and as part of their contract, Alex again has the right to receive contributions from the shop.

iii. In the following year, Alex happens to take a six-month contract with an IT call centre company, and learns that they have an employer pension scheme run by Smart Pensions, to which Alex can also opt in.

There are about a dozen very large pension managers in the UK. Aviva, The People's Pension and Smart Pensions are examples. Between these dozen or so, they have more than a 90% share of the employer pension market, and Alex has now come across three of them.

All employer pension schemes work in the same basic way as follows:

- Once you earn more than a certain threshold amount in a job, the employer/engager is legally obliged to invite you to join their scheme (to *opt in*).

- If you agree, the employer contributes an extra percentage of your fee/salary to the pension scheme, often 3% or thereabouts.

- This is usually conditional on you agreeing to contribute a percentage of your fee to the scheme as well, instead of being paid it in cash. This is often 5% or thereabouts.

> So, say for example that your monthly fee/salary on a job is £2,000. Opting in to the scheme will mean that your employer pays £60 (3%) into your pension on top of your £2,000 fee, but you will have to agree to pay in £100 (5%) from your fee to get that benefit.
>
> Remember that the £100 deducted from your fee will have basic rate tax added back to it automatically by HMRC when it lands in your fund, so it will be worth £125 to your pension fund.
>
> Thus you will only receive £1,900 of your £2,000 fee right now; but you will have £185 paid into your pension on top (less small charges paid to the provider), so your total package is worth £2,085 to you.

Your employer/engager will ask you whether you want to opt in or opt out. With the Equity and MU schemes, once you have joined and opted in the first time, you stay opted in for all future jobs where the engager uses that scheme. When you opt in, the pension provider sends you a login and password for their portal. You keep this account for as long as you keep pension funds with that provider.

It is up to you to keep track of all the different pension funds you have, and all the different logins and passwords. It is absolutely vital that you *stay on top of this*, or you will lose your money. Nobody else does this for you. In autumn 2024, the Pension Policy Institute calculated that there was more than £30 billion in unclaimed, 'lost' pension fund money in the UK. This only happens because people have contributed, and had employers contribute for them, but have then lost track of their account in that fund.

Sometimes people think that in order to avoid the problem of losing track of different funds, it is better to combine or consolidate them into one fund. Alex could choose to do this. For example, when they leave Lauren's shop and do not plan ever to return, they could ask The People's Pension to transfer the fund over to Aviva, since they plan to keep their membership of Aviva's Equity Pension Scheme for their whole career.

But I usually advise against doing this. First, Alex will incur charges in transferring that they will not incur if they keep all pension funds intact. Second, I tend to feel that Alex is on a hiding to nothing if they hope to get through a forty-five- to fifty-year career with only one employer pension portal. It's just not going to happen. There are too many providers and too much flexibility in the market. Alex simply cannot duck the task of keeping a proper record of their various pension accounts from day one to the day of retirement.

So should I always opt in to an employer pension when invited?

There are clearly some distinct advantages:

- If you opt out, you will not receive the employer's extra 3% (Alex's £60 mentioned above). You will simply lose out on the possibility of getting it.

- Always opting in will focus your mind on your overall pension planning.

- You will get the tax benefit of making your own deducted contribution (the £25 Alex got back above by agreeing to pay in his £100).

What are the disadvantages?

- You have to contribute yourself. Alex waves goodbye to £100 in 2026 and won't see it again for fifty years (by which time it will be worth a lot more, but still).

- The Equity Pension Scheme has relatively high charges – Alex could pay lower ones if they paid the same £100 into another scheme.

- You didn't choose your employers' scheme (the employer did) and so if they chose badly, you are not in control of the investment. (But you can counteract this disadvantage by transferring the money after you leave that employer, if you want to.)

- You have to keep track of your portals and logins and passwords for all these different pension pots that you acquire. (But you just do have to. I do not really accept that this creates a reason not to opt in. In effect, you are being paid to undertake this basic task.)

Pension summary

- Pension saving is often a very good idea.

- But you need to pay attention to it from day one, to ensure that the methods you are deploying are the right ones for you and to ensure that you know what is happening to your money and why.

- Only opt out of an employer pension if you are confident about these matters and understand exactly what you are doing as an alternative way of long-term saving.

Mortgages

What is a mortgage?

A mortgage is a large loan from a bank, building society or similar provider to help someone buy a property. Mortgages often last twenty-five years or more.

As we know, Alex rents their home, and pays the landlord monthly rent of £1,000. Alex doesn't buy anything with that money beyond the right to live in the flat for the length of the lease.

Shobu, however, owns her home. She bought it for £400,000. She funded this with a deposit of £30,000 and a mortgage from Nationwide for £370,000. This means that Nationwide gave Shobu's seller £370,000 and now asks Shobu for £1,500 per month for the next twenty-five years. This adds up to *way* more than £370,000, because Shobu has to pay interest on the amount she borrowed, and she also has to pay Nationwide for their time and trouble.

We can see that Shobu has some advantages, while Alex has others. The debate about renting versus owning is a complex one with many aspects to it. It is worth noting that the UK has a very owner-centric culture – most people believe it is preferable to own – compared to the culture in many other countries. About 65% of homes in the UK are owner-occupied, compared to only 40% in, say, Germany.

Let's look at some of the positions, pros and cons in this complex debate.

- **Investment.** Shobu is not simply paying for somewhere to live. She has invested in her own home. Provided her own home becomes more valuable as time goes on (which is the norm in the UK), she receives all the profit when the property is sold for more than the £400,000 she bought it for. Nationwide does not get any of that profit.

- **Climbing the ladder.** Suppose Shobu wants to move to a bigger home in ten years' time, and suppose that in that time the price of her home has gone up from £400,000 to £500,000. She can use the £100,000 as a deposit on the new, larger home, and probably carry on paying the same monthly amount to live in the nicer place. Whereas Alex, if they want to move to a nicer home, will just have to find more rent money from somewhere.

- **Mortgages are eventually paid off.** After twenty-five years, Shobu's mortgage will stop. If she wants to stay on in her home, she can, and she has no monthly cost at all after that – whereas Alex still has to pay rent and go on paying rent for ever.

- **Permission.** Shobu is in charge of her home. If she wants to paint the walls or house ten cats, she can. Alex cannot do these things without their landlord's permission.

- **Maintenance.** On the other hand, Shobu is also responsible for her home. When the loo breaks, she has to pay the plumber to fix it. Alex does not – their landlord does.

- **The interest question.** It costs Shobu the total amount of interest on the life of the mortgage – scores of thousands of pounds over the years – to acquire her property. Alex paid out none of this. Alex could, if they wanted to and if they got sufficiently well organised, have invested the same money in lots of ways that might have resulted in a larger pot.

- **Deposits and partners.** Observe the two significant hurdles that Shobu had to get over, which Alex did not. First, Shobu needed a £30,000 deposit to get started with her first purchase. Some people may have savings, or help from relatives, to achieve this, but many others will not, and saving for a deposit is very difficult. Second, if Shobu's monthly mortgage is more than rent (it may be or it may not be) then she either needs to pay that, or team up with a partner or a lodger to help her bridge the gap.

- **Flexibility.** It is much harder for Shobu to move quickly than it is for Alex, should they need to for work, family or personal reasons.

- **Security.** Alex may rightly be worried about the security of their tenure long-term, if they like their flat and want to stay there. The landlord could decide to sell it whenever they like, and then Alex would have to leave whether they wanted to or not; whereas Shobu keeps her home for as long as she likes. She's in total charge. At the time of writing, the UK is slowly introducing more policies that give tenants a bit more security of tenure than they had before, but the central problem remains – a landlord can decide to sell their property eventually, even if they have to give the tenant some notice.

- **Future checks on income.** Both Alex and Shobu are likely to be subject to checks on their income in future, if they want to move, or in Shobu's case to remortgage (more on this at the end of this section). As long as they keep paying their monthly rent or mortgage when they stay in the same property, their landlord/lender will have no reason to check. But if they want to move, both will be subject to new checks on their income level.

We can see that there are so many aspects to the accommodation debate that we can't really talk about pros and cons in any neat way. What we are looking at here is a series of trade-offs. And each one of us has to consider trade-offs throughout our lives. Certain aspects of financial self-management are no-brainers – pay your NI contributions, for example. Others are more opaque and are really about your personal – and ever-shifting – circumstances. One issue that is outside our scope, for example, is relationships, and then relationships that result in children, and how this impacts on things like pension planning and getting a mortgage, and how relationships and parenthood impact on your career. I'll have to leave it to someone else to write another book about these; but I'm well aware, in setting out these basics, that they are likely to come along one day and force you to change and develop whatever plans you may have made up to that point.

Applying for a mortgage

Let's get back to sorting out Alex's life for them, and imagine that Alex is now weighing up those trade-offs for themselves, and looking into getting a mortgage.

You can apply for a mortgage direct to the provider. Sometimes your own bank is a mortgage lender, and will invite or incentivise you to apply to it. Or you could look at the well-known comparison websites which always offer a huge variety of fast-changing deals.

The fundamental basis of a mortgage application is the proof of your earnings over a period of time, usually three years. The mortgage lenders are governed by quite strict rules and protocols about who they can lend to, in part because the global financial crashes of 1991 and 2008 were to a certain extent caused by 'overexuberant' mortgage-lending.

If you have been employed PAYE in the same job for three or more years, it is easy to present this relative stability to your prospective mortgage lender as a good predictor of your ability to afford the monthly payments going forward.

It is a bit harder for a freelancer to demonstrate the same predictability, because their income is likely to go up and down in a more volatile way, and every contract only lasts a few months and may or may not be followed by another.

You, the creative freelancer, may object to this. The fact that a PAYE employee has been in the same job at the same salary for the past three years is no guarantee that they won't be sacked or made redundant next year, and therefore this system intuitively feels unfair to freelancers. You are absolutely right to feel aggrieved. That's how it goes. Sorry.

Because of this in-built imbalance between employment statuses, a creative freelancer is very likely to benefit from the assistance of a professional mortgage broker, rather than trying to find their way through the thick forest of the mortgage market themselves. Not only will a broker have a comprehensive understanding of the market, but a broker who specialises in self-employed clients will know which mortgagers are likely to be more flexible than others about agreeing your particular earnings.

Some mortgagers work on basic formulae to calculate the amount they will lend you, based on your average earnings over three years. For example, some will usually look to lend you four-and-a-half times your annual earnings if you pay a 10% deposit. Immediately there you will notice two possible variables: the multiple of your earnings, and the size of your deposit. Prospective lenders may well be interested in other variables too, for example:

- How many years you have been self-employed.

- Whether they calculate your average earnings over the last two years or three years – this varies from lender to lender.

- How recent your last tax return is (if you are applying in May, it is unlikely that you have done last year's tax return yet, but if you are applying in December then you probably have).

- If you are presenting an existing contract as evidence of future earnings – say that Shobu has a contract on a TV soap – different lenders may place different weight on it, and may be interested in the length and the terms.

As you can see, this can get very complicated very quickly, and so I tend to recommend using a mortgage broker because they should have a very thorough knowledge of the fast-changing market and the differing requirements of different lenders. There are several specialist mortgage brokers for creative freelancers.

Can I understate my expenses in order to increase my mortgage lending?

You may by now have spotted a curious opposition between two aspects of our discussions to this point.

A self-employed person might be motivated to deduct as *many* expenses as possible, so that they can reduce their tax bill.

But the same person might also be motivated to deduct as *few* expenses as possible, so that their net earnings are higher, a mortgage-lender agrees to lend them more, and they get to buy a bigger flat in a nicer neighbourhood. (Or any flat at all, if their challenge is reporting enough income to be accepted for a mortgage full stop.)

Let's suppose that in 2028, after three full years of typical creative self-employment mixed with a bit of PAYE on the side, Alex decides to try to get on the housing ladder. We already know that in 2025/26 they reported taxable earnings of £18,800. Let's say that in 2026/27 this increased to £25,000.

Alex is now considering their tax return for 2027/28. They had a stronger year than before, with £35,000 of fee income from all their different kinds of acting and teaching. They calculate their expenses in the same way as previous years and with careful reference to all the advice in Chapter 4, and come up with an expenses total of £5,000, meaning they would report earnings of £35,000 - £5,000 = £30,000. (Remember that the lender is interested in Alex's profit, their income minus their expenses – not just their income. The lender is thinking of Alex's profit as a self-employed person's 'salary'.)

Suppose that Alex has begun talking to a mortgage broker who advises that they are likely to be able to borrow four times their average earnings over the two years before the application. As things stand, therefore, Alex will be able to borrow a mortgage of:

£25,000 (Earlier year earnings)
+
£30,000 (Latest year earnings)

= £55,000

÷ 2 = £27,500

x 4 = £110,000

Alex can see that if they claim say £3,000 fewer expenses in 2027/28, their borrowing power will increase, because now their average earnings increase to £29,000 and so their borrowing power increases to £116,000.

If Alex is thinking of choosing not to deduct expenses which they could have deducted, in order to increase their borrowing, there are two downsides:

i. They will pay £600 more tax in 2027/28, because of the £3,000 of deductible expenses which have not been claimed.

ii. Although HMRC will never object to taxpayers under-deducting expenses and paying more tax, the mortgage lender might do so if they look closely enough. Some mortgage lenders will ask to see Alex's tax return. If Alex has claimed, for example, far lower travel expenses in 2027/28 than they did in 2026/27, despite making more income, then the mortgage lender might ask why, and Alex will be unlikely to have a good answer.

This is a tricky matter on which to offer very definite advice, and in practice everyone will need to come to their own decision about this. On the one hand, it is illegal and dishonest to misrepresent your earnings to a mortgage lender. On the other hand, it is not illegal nor dishonest to decide that you will not claim a deduction for a cup of coffee bought at the café during rehearsals which you could have claimed if you'd wanted, with the consequence that you report a tax return with a higher profit and pay more income tax. This is just one of those very difficult paths and balancing acts that the creative freelancer must find their way through.

Mortgage rates and remortgaging

I deliberately painted an oversimplified picture, on page 146, in my example about Shobu's Nationwide mortgage that lasts twenty-five years.

In fact it is very rare indeed for someone to keep the same mortgage for twenty-five years. Most mortgages include the ability and indeed the expectation that the deal initially signed will change within a relatively small number of years, so that a few years after you buy a property, you remortgage.

One of the reasons for this is the relationship between the two most common types of mortgage: *fixed-rate* and *variable-rate*.

With a fixed-rate mortgage, you and the lender agree that, for a period of time (often one, two or five years) you will pay an agreed fixed interest rate. At the end of that period, you will be free either to renegotiate the rate or to move ('port') your mortgage to another lender, if you can find one to agree to take you on, and if you pay a modest transfer fee (which it may well be worth your while to do when the time comes).

With a standard variable-rate mortgage, the rate you pay is tied to the interest rate set by the Bank of England. The Bank of England committee meets every month to decide whether to move the rate up or down, or to leave it unchanged; you may have seen this monthly meeting covered in the news. If they move it up or down, most people's variable-rate mortgages sync up or down instantly, which is why there is so much attention paid to these monthly meetings.

The advantage of a fixed-rate mortgage is that you know exactly what you will pay for the length of the fix, and you can accordingly budget with certainty; with a variable rate, you might find that rates go up and you suddenly have to pay more. This difficult situation cannot possibly happen to a person with a fixed-rate mortgage or indeed to a tenant paying rent – they know exactly what they will pay for the length of the contract.

On the other hand, a variable-rate mortgage is usually offered slightly more cheaply. And you may be a keen observer of politics and economics, and perhaps you think that interest rates are likely to go down over the coming months and years. In that case, you might prefer to take a variable rate and bet on the possibility that interest rates go down and you start paying less every month. This benefit cannot come to someone on a fixed-rate mortgage, nor to a tenant paying rent.

Also, many lenders advertise a special offer of X% fixed for Y years, or maybe a discount of Z% from their current standard variable rate. After that, if you do not remortgage, the rate drops back on to the standard variable rate again. When you remortgage or arrange a new mortgage deal with your current lender, you are asking to be accepted for their latest 'special offer'. If you have your ducks in a row and can pass all the checks they require, you can essentially stay on the mortgage lender's special offer rates for ever, and minimise the amount of interest you pay them for the loan of their money.

This is very complex and difficult choice, and you might well take the view that it presents another good reason to try to work with a mortgage broker, because they will probably understand the ins and outs of these choices better than you do, and will be likely to be in a position to offer you good advice.

In practice, as a homeowner, Shobu will simply have to engage with this issue every three to five years at least, because mortgage rates and economic circumstances tend to change a good deal in that timeframe. If Shobu does not remortgage, she will end up paying more for her mortgage over its long life than she needs to.

Shobu also needs to consider her income each time she remortgages or moves house. If it's lower than it was, she may not be able to move to a mortgage lender with a lower rate than her current lender offers, or may not be able to move to the house she would like to buy. Shobu has to try to make sure her income either stays the same or has a steady rise in line with inflation to give herself the best chance of a streamlined mortgage/remortgage application, and this is, of course, difficult in the freelancing world.

Savings

We have seen that Alex's monthly budget is pretty tight, and doesn't allow much room for the possibility of saving. For many people in the creative industries, this will be the reality of trying to forge or continue a creative career, perhaps especially in London where the cost of living is high.

If possible, however, Alex should try to save wherever possible, especially if extra dollops of cash come in from time to time such as, for example, gifts from family members at birthday-time, and any other unexpected windfalls.

Options for saving

An ISA (Individual Savings Account) is a very popular first port of call for savings. You can pay up to a certain limit into an ISA every year (£20,000 at the time of writing). Your bank will almost certainly offer ISAs, or you can look for one with a trusted name using the comparison websites. All will offer you different deals, special offers, etc., but this is a relatively easy choice to make by yourself, unlike the choice of a mortgage.

The best thing about ISAs is that you never, ever pay tax on the money that is earned in your ISA, with no ceiling on the amount you can earn and no time-limit to that benefit. This is different to savings you have in an ordinary account or fund or portfolio, in two ways:

i. In another type of account, if you earn interest income, or dividend income from money invested in companies, then you pay tax on those earnings as you go along.

ii. If you invest in shares in companies, either on your own or through a fund or savings account, then you pay Capital Gains Tax on the increase in value of the shares when you sell them.

But neither of these things happen in an ISA. You could, for example, put money into an ISA which buys shares on your behalf in Flying Taxis Ltd, a startup. Those shares could be sold for one million pounds in ten years' time. If they are held in your ISA, you will pay not one penny in tax on that one million pounds. But if you had bought the shares directly from Flying Taxis Ltd, and sold them for the same amount ten years later, you would pay 18% to 24% Capital Gains Tax at current rates.

Other building society or savings accounts or fixed-term bonds can also be useful, especially for saving in the short-term. Again, you can find the best deals on comparison websites and you can save as much as you like without limit. You may well be offered a better interest rate if you agree to lock your money in for a short period, say a year or three years, or if you agree that you will have a period of notice before you withdraw money, say three months. In these accounts, however, you pay annual income tax on the amount of interest that you earn.

Cash ISAs (as opposed to stocks-and-shares ISAs, which are higher-risk) and other building society accounts are very low-risk investments. You will probably not get the best possible rate of return on your savings, but they will never lose your money (and indeed the government guarantees it up to a certain amount).

You can find more sophisticated investment platforms on the comparison websites, or on crowd-funding platforms, all offering different methods and formats for investment, many offering different risk profiles. These may make better returns. There are also some tax breaks for certain types of investment in startup companies. But, as you always hear on the adverts, the value of such investments can go down as well as up. They might lose your money.

Bear in mind that pensions, which we covered in detail earlier in this chapter, are another type of saving. You should always consider pension saving as part of your overall savings strategy, albeit being aware that you are tying your money up for a long time, as opposed to using an ISA or a building society account where you can get at your savings whenever you want.

Insurance

Everyone will be familiar with the concept of car, home or pet insurance: you pay the insurers an annual or monthly premium, and they pay you if something goes wrong like an accident, a flood or a sore paw.

Now, though, let's look at three other types of insurance that you should consider as part of your overall financial strategy. All these types of insurance can be researched and bought via the comparison websites.

Life insurance

Not the cheeriest topic, but something you may need to consider. You pay an annual or monthly premium, and they pay out to your nominated beneficiary if you die before a specified age, or if you have a terminal illness and do not have long to live.

Whether or not you will be interested in this product depends on your personal circumstances. Alex, as we have seen, is living on their own, has no children and hardly any property, so there is not much point in them paying out a life insurance premium for now. Khalil, however, is married with two young children. His wife is a part-time nurse and would be in an impossible financial position if Khalil died suddenly, particularly if he did so while the children are still dependents; and so life insurance feels like an absolute must for him.

Income protection insurance

PAYE employees generally have some kind of safety net protecting a proportion of their income in the event that they fall sick. They certainly benefit from Statutory Sick Pay at the very least, a basic amount that the government refunds to their employer so that the employer can pass it on to the sick employee (funded by National Insurance). And many companies, especially larger ones, offer more generous benefits to employees who are off sick for a while.

A self-employed person, by contrast, has no such safety net. And therefore you may want to consider income protection insurance, which will pay you a basic 'wage' in the event that you cannot work because of sickness.

It is very hard to advise whether this kind of policy is generally a good idea or not. Realistically, you need a crystal ball to know if it is or not: because if you never have to use it, you'll think it was a waste of money that you had it, whereas if you do have to use it over a long period of time, you'll thank your lucky stars that you bought it.

If you have been ill before you start your self-employment, or if you have a disability, you will need to disclose this if you want to buy income protection insurance, and this may affect the premium you pay, or possibly the insurer may refuse to cover you for a condition that you had before you applied to buy a policy.

Private health insurance

This is a more straightforward choice. Some people decide to pay a monthly fee to companies such as BUPA or AXA, which then function like a sort of 'private NHS' – you can get all the services you would usually expect to get from a doctor or a hospital, only from the private sections rather than the NHS sections.

There are very widely differing opinions about whether this is a sensible use of cash, and there are also the same kinds of moral issues with this type of service that apply to, say, the issue of private education: we could debate (in another book) whether this type of service is harmful to society or not, in creating effectively a 'two-tier' system for provisions that everybody needs.

Benefits

The benefit system in the UK is complex, and the rules around different kinds of benefits change frequently. Here I give an overview of some of the most common types of benefit, but if you believe you may qualify for any or some of these you will need to undertake further research.

There are lots of sources of information about benefits, and the Citizens Advice Bureau (www.citizensadvice.org.uk) may be a good place to start. If you have a disability, then there are sometimes organisations that are experts in the particular field of your disability, and engaging with these is a must. Most benefits are applied for and paid via the Department for Work and Pensions (DWP).

Universal Credit (UC)

Universal Credit is the most common type of benefit. You generally qualify for it if you are not in work and if you have less than a certain level of savings. If, in August 2025, Alex had not been able to find the work in Lauren's shop that we described, or any other casual PAYE work; and if they had had a slow start to their income from acting work, then they may have qualified for UC.

You apply online for UC to the DWP. How much you may receive is on a sliding scale depending on various personal criteria.

UC requires you to file a mini-'return' every month via the DWP website to confirm how much, if any, income you have received. If you are self-employed and trying to get your own business going, the UC 'return' also asks you to state what expenses you have incurred for your business in that month, in much the same sense we discussed in relation to the tax return in Chapter 4.

If you are paid UC for a long time, you may find that the DWP introduces extra conditions on you as regards the type of work you want to accept. For example, they might allow you some leeway in choosing not to apply for jobs that come up at a library or a leisure centre, early in your claim period – but then later on, insist that you apply for these, under threat of losing your UC if you do not.

UC income is not reportable on your tax return and is not taxed.

Jobseekers' Allowance

If you have made sufficient National Insurance contributions over some years, and if you then have a period of unemployment, you may qualify for Jobseekers' Allowance rather than UC. This is a more generous benefit, designed for slightly older people who are more likely to be 'between jobs', than to be experiencing long periods of low-paid employment or self-employment.

Jobseekers' Allowance is reportable on your tax return and is taxed.

PIP and Access to Work

PIP and Access to Work are grants to help people with disabilities. The DWP assesses them and pays them out on an individual basis, and after complex application procedures.

These benefits are not reportable or taxable.

Child Benefit

Child Benefit, like the State Pension, is not means-tested: it is paid (by HMRC) to everyone who cares for a child under 18 years old.

However, there is a mechanism by which all or some of it is clawed back if you earn more than £60,000 per year, or if your partner does, in the case of a two-parent household. Apply online to HMRC when you begin being responsible for a child, but bear in mind that if your income goes over that threshold, you will have to pay some or all of the money back at the end of the year.

Working tax credits and child tax credits

These are, in effect, additional Child benefits which *are* means-tested and are paid only to those who need them, via HMRC and upon application online. These benefits are not reportable or taxable on your tax return.

Tax-free childcare

If you have a pre-school-age child, and if you and your partner earn between the minimum wage and £100,000 per year, then you are entitled to have £2,000 per year of your bill for registered childminders or nurseries reimbursed to you by HMRC. Unlike Child Benefit, this is not dealt with on your tax return: you have a special section within your HMRC account online which deals with it.

Maternity Allowance (MA)

PAYE employees who are on Maternity Leave usually benefit from a package of support from their employer. Smaller employers usually look to have a large part of the cost of this reimbursed by the DWP, whereas larger employers may offer you quite generous benefits from their own pocket because they want to encourage you to return afterwards, and can afford to do so because they are bigger companies.

Here again, of course, the self-employed are in a different position, so they need to apply to the DWP for a State benefit called Maternity Allowance. MA is not reportable on your tax return and is not taxable, but there may be restrictions on how many hours per week you can work at the time you are receiving it, so if you do plan to work a few hours, you should check these rules carefully.

Housing benefit or local housing allowance

If you receive UC and some other kinds of benefits, you may also be eligible for help with rental costs – check the rules on these by searching for them on www.gov.uk if you think they may apply to you.

Golden rules for pensions, mortgages, savings, insurance and benefits

- You should save into a pension scheme unless you have a very well-informed and thought-through reason not to.

- You should almost certainly opt in to any employer pension scheme offered to you.

- Understand your pension strategy, and make sure you keep all your logins and passwords to all the pension schemes you join throughout your working life.

- Carefully consider whether renting or owning property is best for you. If you want to buy, you will probably benefit from using a specialist mortgage broker.

- Once you have a mortgage, do not expect to simply sit with it for twenty-five to thirty years; you will need to remortgage after a few years.

- An ISA should probably be the first type of savings account you use when you start saving.
- Think about protection insurances as part of your overall strategy.
- Always consider and check what State benefits you might be eligible for.

6. VAT and Limited Companies

Now that Alex has got to grips with the financial basics of their life as a sole trader, it's time to delve a little further into some more complex business issues. Alex is going to need at least to consider these points. They may or may not need to act on them: that depends on how their career develops.

What is VAT?

Value Added Tax (VAT) is a different type of tax to income tax. It is a *sales* tax. Consumers and private individuals do not have any choice about paying it; it is automatically added to any bill we pay that requires it. We all pay VAT on some goods and services we choose to buy, for the simple reason that it helps the government raise more money. Some businesses, however, have a choice about paying it or not.

The VAT system sits *alongside* the Income Tax system that we discussed in Chapters 2–4. It is something you need to consider additionally and separately.

Let's consider three different types of customers who buy something. I'm going to label these i), ii) and iii).

i. A private individual.

ii. A business, regardless of its legal structure – I will have more to say about different structures later, but by 'legal structure' I mean, for example, either a sole trader freelancer like Alex, or a Limited Company like Lauren's Shoreditch shop – that makes sales of *less* than £90,000 in any year.

iii. A business, regardless of its legal structure, that makes sales of *more* than £90,000 in any year.

And now let's consider three different types of things they buy, which I'm going to label A, B and C.

A. Most *goods* and *services* that are supplied to a customer based in the UK. 'Goods' would include lots of everyday objects, like a pencil that you buy in a stationery shop, or a new computer. 'Services' would include ongoing relationships that you want to buy into, such as a phone contract (so, for example, you see that VAT shows on your phone bill), and things like the fee that Alex charges to a producer for appearing in a show.

B. A small number of goods and services which by law do *not* attract VAT: this applies to, for example, staple foods, printed newspapers, books and bank charges.

C. Goods and services bought from a supplier based outside the UK.

This table shows the VAT position for each type of customer buying each type of supply, so cross-relating our i), ii) and iii) to our A, B and C.

	i) Private individual	ii) Business (less than £90,000 sales)	iii) Business (more than £90,000 sales)
A. Most UK goods and services	The customer pays VAT at 20%. For normal purchases in a shop, the VAT is included in the price. The only way you know it's there is if you look at the receipt. So, if you pay £1 for a pencil in WH Smith, the actual cost was 83.3p plus 16.7p VAT.* For some kinds of purchases, often services that you buy from larger companies, you will notice that they quote the price to you already separating the two elements. For example, a solicitor might tell you they charge £200 + VAT per hour, so you pay them £240.	Can choose either not to register for VAT, and be like column i), or to register for VAT, and be like column iii). So the seeming advantage of a sole trader business registering for VAT, even if the business takes less than £90,000 a year, is that you can reclaim all the VAT the business is charged on its expenses. (I'll come back to this.)	This business must be VAT-registered, because it has exceeded the £90,000 threshold. It reclaims all the VAT it is charged on expenses.

B. Basics that do not attract VAT	No VAT is charged on these sorts of goods and supplies. There is not much strong rationale behind this. It used to be a concession for items that are regarded as 'essential', but that definition has weakened over time. Now it just is what it is.	See column i. No VAT is charged.	See column i. No VAT is charged.

A private individual *suffers* VAT; this means that they pay it out, they lose it. There's no meaningful distinction to them between the net price of the goods and the VAT.

A private individual cannot register for VAT unless they are a sole trader business, like Alex. VAT registration is a concept that only applies to businesses.

	Or, of course, you might buy something from a small, non-VAT-registered business that would be VATable if a larger business sold it, but it is not because a smaller business sells it. A cup of coffee, for example, is VATable at Starbucks, but not VATable at Vanessa's Coffee Van, because Vanessa only runs her van from 7 a.m. to 10 a.m. weekdays and is not big enough to want to be VAT-registered.		
C. Goods and services from outside the UK	The overseas supplier charges you VAT in their own country, and again you just have to pay it.	The overseas supplier may or may not charge UK VAT, usually depending on its size. The UK business customer can either choose to be VAT-	The overseas supplier may or may not charge UK VAT, usually depending on its size. The UK VAT-registered business can reclaim any UK VAT charged.

	registered and reclaim any UK VAT charged, or to remain unregistered and suffer any VAT charged.	

---

* The way I calculated the breakdown between the main pencil cost and the VAT was to divide the £1 by 1.2. Don't interrogate this, just do it. (Or if you really want to interrogate it, go and take Maths A-Level, and rather you than me.) It is a common error to do this sum in your head and come up with the answer that the pencil must cost 80p and the VAT is 20p. But 20p is not 25% of 80p. It is 25% of 80p. The VAT rate is 20%, not 25%. You aren't looking for one-fifth of the gross price, you are looking for the net price + 20%. Don't overthink this. Just divide the gross price by 1.2 to get the split between net price and VAT.

We'll review this issue below, using the example of Alex's guitar lessons, when we get there (on page 177).

By the way, the price of something including VAT is often called the *gross* price and the price of something excluding the VAT is often called the *net* price. Unfortunately, the words 'gross' and 'net' are also sometimes used to describe things going on with a price that are not to do with VAT. To help avoid this confusion, you will sometimes notice suppliers use the words 'including VAT' or 'excluding VAT', or perhaps they may quote you a price '+ VAT'. This is less confusing.

★ ★ ★

Looking at the table above, you can see that a VAT-registered business appears to have a gigantic advantage over a private consumer and a non-VAT-registered business – it reclaims all the VAT it is charged. Every pencil costs it 83p, not £1.

What's the catch?

The catch is that while the VAT-registered business is *reclaiming* VAT on its costs, it is also *charging* VAT on the goods and services it supplies, and therefore having to send this VAT to HMRC. Let's look at what this means for a creative freelancer.

So-Yeon: the position after compulsory VAT registration

Consider the case of So-Yeon, a sole trader actor who has been VAT-registered for some years. So-Yeon originally became VAT-registered because she had a regular role in a TV soap, and earned more than £100,000 from that job every year for several years.

So So-Yeon was obliged to become VAT-registered because she went over the VAT threshold; she must now *add* VAT to her fees, and pass that back to HMRC; and she can *reclaim* any VAT she is charged on business expenses. So-Yeon cannot hold onto the VAT she charges others; it is not income for her, it is a sales tax that she owes to the Treasury. In effect So-Yeon is a kind of tax collector for HMRC, by being VAT-registered. The only advantage to her is her ability to reclaim the VAT she spends on some expenses.

Let's break this down. Let's imagine that So-Yeon has a week in which she does one TV shoot and charges one fee of £1,000. She has few business expenses that week, except that i) her agent took commission, which is a business expense, and ii) she bought a packet of pencils, which cost £5.

So-Yeon's agent bills the TV producer for £1,000 + VAT (because So-Yeon is registered for VAT). The VAT is £200, i.e. 20% of £1,000. So the producer pays So-Yeon £1,200, via the agent. But So-Yeon isn't going to pocket £1,200 at the end of the day.

So-Yeon's agent deducts their own 12.5% commission, because this is how agents make their living (12.5% of £1,000 = £125) + VAT (because the agent is also a VAT-registered business – £125 x 20% = £25) and so So-Yeon's agent pays So-Yeon £1,200 (what the

TV producer paid, plus VAT) - £150 (what the agent charged So-Yeon, plus VAT) = £1,050.

So-Yeon now owes HMRC the original VAT on her fee (that's £200) *minus* the VAT she is allowed to reclaim as a business expense.

So she *doesn't* have to give HMRC the £25 VAT her agent added to her agent commission, and she can deduct 83p VAT on the pencils, because they are also a business expense (£5 ÷ 1.2 = £4.17, meaning that the VAT charged on the pencils was 83p).

She's reclaiming the VAT that others have charged her, while paying HMRC the VAT on what she has charged others.

So, she pays HMRC £200 - £25 - £0.83 = £174.17.

So-Yeon is left with:

£1,050 (what her agent sent her) - £5 (spent on the pencils) - £174.17 (paid to HMRC) = £870.83.

If she had *not* been VAT-registered, she would have been left with £1,000 (fee) - £150 (agent charge) - £5 (spent on the pencils) = £845.

So we see that, even though VAT registration confers on So-Yeon the obligation to collect VAT on her sales, it actually works in her favour financially, because she is able to reclaim the VAT on her expenses.

Alex: considering choosing to register even if they aren't obliged to

Alex and So-Yeon meet in the green room over a cuppa one day and, since it's raining outside and they both know their lines, they fall to talking about this matter. Alex has grasped the concept of reclaiming VAT and is wondering if they should choose to register voluntarily, according to column ii) in the table above.

We already know that Alex will not reach the threshold this year and so be obliged to register without any choice, but they should consider whether there is any advantage to registering voluntarily. (Remember that Alex can do this because they are a self-employed business; they could not do it if they were a private, PAYE-employed individual.)

The obvious advantage to Alex in choosing to register is that they will, just like So-Yeon, save money: the amount of the VAT they will have to pay HMRC will be less than the amount of the VAT that producers pay them, and they can pocket the difference.

There are, nevertheless, three disadvantages.

i. **Admin.** Registering for and maintaining a VAT system at least *doubles* the amount of book-keeping and form-filling that your business requires, perhaps more. It adds a layer of complexity to Alex's activities which they must be able to cope with. Furthermore, the standard of record-keeping required for VAT is higher than the standard required for a normal income tax return. If Alex is to be VAT-registered, they must scrupulously keep and file every single VAT receipt they receive.

ii. **Obligation to charge VAT to non-VAT registered customers.** Alex does the tour of *Sleeping Beauty* with Laurence Olivier Productions Ltd, which is a large UK-wide producer. Any large producer will be VAT-registered, and therefore does not care whether Alex is or not; they will claim back the VAT paid to Alex in full, because paying Alex is a business expense for them, so this does not increase their costs.

But if Alex later does a play with Sophie & Tim Productions, a small partnership which is *not* VAT-registered, the dynamics will be different. That business *cannot* reclaim VAT paid to Alex. If Alex is not VAT-registered, then their fee with Sophie & Tim is just £1,000, but if Alex is VAT-registered, it becomes £1,200. It may therefore be that Alex looks like a less attractive casting proposition to Sophie & Tim: Alex costs more because of the VAT status.

This also applies to Alex's guitar lessons, given to children. Their parents are paying £20 per lesson. If Alex registers for VAT, the price will need to go up to £24, or Alex will need to continue taking £20 but will have to pay £3.33 VAT on that.

Let's review why the VAT in this example is £4 if Alex charges it to the parents, but only £3.33 if Alex decides to absorb the pain for themselves. It is because the net price is different in the two cases. If Alex adds VAT to the existing price, then the sum is £20 + (20% of £20 is £4) £4 = £24. But if Alex decides to absorb, then the sum to find the new net price is £20 ÷ 1.2 = £16.67, and the VAT is the leftover £3.33.

In practice here, some halfway house between the two, that splits this cost between Alex and the guitar customers, might be the best solution. For example, Alex could put the price the parents pay up to £22 and suffer VAT of £1.67 (because £22 ÷ 1.2 = £18.33, which is what Alex will now actually take home instead of £20).

iii. **Digital book-keeping system.** The only way to file VAT returns is through a digital book-keeping system like Xero or QuickBooks. Back in Chapter 2, we discussed record-keeping and the choices Alex has for this; if VAT-registered, then they have *no* choice. They have to go for the relatively expensive digital book-keeping solution.

How can Alex judge whether the advantage outweighs the disadvantages? I usually advise that a rule-of-thumb to apply here, if you work through an agent, is the '40,000 rule'. If you tend to make at least £40,000 gross income, through an agent, every year, then you should register for VAT voluntarily.

If you have £40,000 gross income, then your agent is charging you commission of £5,000 or £6,000 per year. The great majority of agents are VAT-registered, so that means that if you are not VAT-registered, you are losing at least £1,000 in VAT on commission that you cannot reclaim, but which you could reclaim if you were VAT-registered, even before you consider the extra VAT that you could reclaim on those pencils, hotel bills and coffees in Starbucks.

A cushion of £1,000 should be plenty to offset the inconvenience of the extra admin, and the book-keeping costs. So you will save money if you voluntarily VAT-register once you go past £40,000 income per year billed through your agent.

However, even applying my suggested rule-of-thumb may leave you with some doubts and difficulties:

- If you do not do all your work through an agent, or if your agent is not VAT-registered, then the benefit is less clear.

- If you have a lot of non-VAT-registered customers – for example, if you are working a lot for private individuals, or very small companies – then you may cause yourself a lot of difficulty in trying to collect VAT from these customers.

- You may not earn £40,000 consistently every year. You may dip between, say, £30,000 and £50,000 from year to year. In the £30,000 years you may not see much benefit from being VAT-registered, if any, and you cannot dip in and out of being VAT-registered.

Let's leave Alex wrestling with this complex choice and consider the mechanics of how VAT works in practice.

VAT registration and timing

Alex can register for VAT online at HMRC's website if they decide to do so voluntarily, or in the month in which they pass the threshold of '£90,000 income within the past twelve months', which triggers compulsory VAT registration.

Three important things to note here:

- The £90,000 threshold is an *income* threshold, not a *profit* threshold. Alex's expenses, agent commission, etc. are irrelevant to passing this threshold or not. It is purely about how much in total their engagers and customers paid Alex.

- Only fees and sales count towards the £90,000. If Alex had received a *grant* from the Arts Council, or a *donation* from a charity towards producing a project, that would not count (you would be right to find this a bit confusing, because we noted in Chapter 3 that grants for making work *do* count towards your income tax thresholds – but not for VAT).

- The twelve-month period in which to calculate and judge the income threshold means *any twelve months counting back from the moment you pass £90,000*, not the twelve months of the tax year, the calendar year, the lunar year, the football season, or any other period. So, suppose Alex completes the 25/26 tax year on 5 April 2026 with income of £25,000, and then in July 2026 they suddenly, unexpectedly land a big TV role and are paid a fee of £75,000 over three months, July to September 2026. Exciting times! Alex needs to sit down and calculate their cumulative income *from each twelve-month period* running up to July, then August, then September 2026, in order to see *which* 2026 month is the one in which they go over the £90,000 income threshold for the previous twelve months. Alex is then obliged to register for VAT immediately. They should not wait until the end of 2026/27 to see that their income for the whole of 2026/27 has gone over the £90,000. This is too late. So if you think you may be in this position, it is critical to calculate at the end of every month, in real time, how much you have made over the twelve months *to that month-end*.

If Alex does get into this situation and misses the deadline, and does not realise until the summer of 2027 that they should have registered for VAT much earlier, all is not lost, although they will have to pay an irritating penalty to HMRC upon eventually registering. This is why it is essential to get out in front of this problem, and begin to consider VAT registration as soon as you get a very well-paid contract. I do not want to say anything against agents – some of my best friends are agents – but as a breed, they tend not to be very good at advising their clients to look out for this issue when that first big role comes in. So watch out for this when it does.

VAT returns

We looked above at a simple example of So-Yeon's VAT position over a single week, and we saw that she would be a few pounds better off over the week by being VAT-registered.

In fact, VAT returns are not made weekly, thank goodness, but quarterly. Your VAT quarter can end in any month, but the vast majority of VAT-registered people align their VAT quarters with the tax year, so that they submit their returns for the quarters to June, September, December and March.

The deadline for submitting every quarterly VAT return is the month after the end of the quarter, so if your VAT quarter ended in June, you must submit your VAT return by the end of July, and this is also the deadline for paying over any VAT that you have collected on HMRC's behalf, minus, of course, the VAT you are reclaiming on your expenses.

There are modest penalties for submitting your VAT return late, and for paying a few days late: these begin to multiply painfully after a couple of weeks, so you cannot be too blasé about VAT deadlines.

It is possible to submit a VAT return for a period in which HMRC owes *you* money, rather than you owing them.

Suppose that Alex has been between gigs for a whole quarter, and has been working PAYE in the shop or the call centre. Or suppose the only work they have done in the quarter was a shoot overseas, invoiced to an overseas TV company. In both these cases, Alex may well not have collected any VAT on *fees* (if you are being paid PAYE, you are not yourself a business; if you are being paid by an overseas contractor, you do not charge UK VAT). But they will still have paid out VAT on *expenses* like their phone bill and their Netflix subscription. And so in that quarter, they will make a 'minus' VAT return, and HMRC will pay the VAT that Alex is reclaiming by direct credit to Alex's bank account. It's a bit like solar power on your roof, transferring energy back into the National Grid.

Book-keeping for VAT

If you are VAT-registered, you cannot keep your books and records in any way other than by using a cloud-based app such as Xero or QuickBooks: no more spreadsheets. (Unfortunately, SansDrama does not support VAT.) You can still keep paper receipts if you like, or you can upload them to your app as you go along so that everything is in one place, but the transactions must all be recorded on an app. Your VAT returns are made directly from the app.

This means that anyone who is VAT-registered will not have to worry much about compliance with Making Tax Digital, the self-assessment change we discussed in Chapter 2: they will already be compliant.

The receipts regime for VAT is much stricter than the receipts regime for income tax. Suppose that HMRC enquire into So-Yeon's affairs. So-Yeon has claimed the expense of a haircut on 17 July, noted in her records. She has claimed the expense on her income tax return, and also, because her hairdresser is VAT-registered and charges VAT, claimed back the VAT on her VAT return.

First, So-Yeon has an enquiry from an *income tax, self-assessment* inspector. The inspector asks to see the receipt for the 17 July haircut, and So-Yeon cannot produce it because she lost it. But she can produce other evidence of it, for example:

- She shows the inspector her credit card statement, where on that date there is a transaction showing at the hairdresser's.

- She also shows him an email from her agent dated 16 July, in which her agent says 'I know that Patti, who you are meeting tomorrow, is fanatical about hairdos, so do get your hair done in the morning.'

The inspector is not *obliged* to accept these pieces of evidence as proof of allowability, but in my experience they would be very likely to do so.

But next, So-Yeon has an enquiry from a *VAT inspector*. The VAT inspector will not accept any proof of the expense other than a VAT receipt; no ifs, no buts. Triple affidavits from the King, Benedict Cumberbatch and Emma Raducanu would not persuade the inspector to allow it.

So, you need to be obsessive about collecting receipts when you are VAT-registered.

VAT Flat Rate scheme

Lastly, before we leave VAT, a word about the Flat Rate scheme.

The Flat Rate scheme is a simplified VAT system, designed to help smaller sole traders be VAT-registered with a lighter burden on their paperwork.

Under the Flat Rate scheme, instead of charging 20% VAT to your customers, paying that over to HMRC, and reclaiming 20% VAT on your expenses, you do something different. You pay over a smaller percentage to HMRC and you do not claim any expenses – you keep the difference between the 20% that you charged your customers and the lower rate that HMRC sets for your particular profession.

The rate for actors used to be 12%, and so some years ago it worked to the advantage of many actors to be on the Flat Rate scheme because they actually got more VAT back from their quarterly returns than if they had taken the trouble to itemise all their expenses, fanatically keep all their expense receipts, etc.

However, a few years ago the Flat Rate for actors was effectively increased to 16.5%, and so nowadays I tend to advise actors that they will be better off ignoring the Flat Rate scheme and processing their VAT in the full way.

The advent of Making Tax Digital shores up this advice: you will now have to keep a digital record of every expense as it is, so one of the main former advantages of the Flat Rate scheme, where you could have lighter-touch book-keeping, is gone now anyway.

A final note: we noted in Chapter 3 that trivial corrections to Income Tax returns are very easily made, but a stricter regime applies to making corrections to VAT returns, so if you are doing your own VAT returns, make sure you are well informed about this.

Golden rules for VAT

- Think about registering voluntarily if you are billing about £40,000+ through an agent.

- Think about VAT urgently as soon as you secure a very well-paid gig.

- VAT is a pain to get your head round, and it forces you into stricter book-keeping, but in the long run this actually helps you to keep everything clear and well-ordered.

- Keep receipts, keep receipts, keep receipts, and then after that make sure you keep receipts. Did I also mention that you need to keep receipts?

★ ★ ★

Now it's time to consider the issue of Limited Companies.

Limited Companies

In our discussions so far, all the creative freelancers we have looked at are 'sole traders'. As we have seen, this means that they are private individuals who have told HMRC that they are in business as self-employed people.

When Laurence Olivier Productions engaged Alex for the tour, they contracted with Alex personally as a sole trader.

But you will have noticed that, every day, you have dealings with businesses that are not like this. When you go into Tesco and buy a loaf of bread, you are contracting with Tesco, not with Ken Murphy personally (he is the Chief Exec of Tesco).

This is because every business has a *choice* about what legal structure to choose. 'Sole tradership' is only one of these structures, and now we are going to look at the other most common structure, a Limited Company.

A Limited Company is a legal entity in its own right. Alex's sole tradership is not separable from Alex themselves. There's only one Alex. But if Alex forms a Limited Company, Alex Actor Limited (or 'Ltd'), there are now two entities to consider, Alex personally and the separate company.

A Limited Company must have two other sorts of entities as constituents:

i. Shareholders (**or** '**members**') – These are the people (or other companies) who *own* the company.

ii. Directors – These are the people who are *in charge of operating* the company.

It is common to have companies in which these two groups of people are exactly the same people, and equally common not to. It depends on the company. If Alex decides to form Alex Actor Ltd to operate their business, from everything we know about them we can say that it would probably be sensible for them to be the only shareholder and the only Director of their company. On the other hand, while Ken Murphy is both a shareholder and a Director of Tesco, there are also thousands and thousands of other shareholders as well (you might be one, or your pension fund might be one without you even realising), and about a dozen other Directors. This distinction happens simply because Tesco is a much larger and more complicated company than Alex Actor Ltd.

A company's ownership ('capital') comprises shares which can be bought and sold, and which change value. (This is not always the case and we'll look at some alternatives in the next chapter, but share capital is the norm.)

If Alex forms Alex Actor Ltd tomorrow, based on what we know about their business, the shares in their company will not be worth anything (or rather, only the common nominal amount of £1). A share in Tesco, by contrast, can be bought on the day I am writing this for £4 on the London Stock Exchange. Google is a much more valuable company, and a share in Google can be bought on the day I am writing this on the Nasdaq exchange in the USA for $173.

So when a Limited Company is in business, something different is happening to when a sole trader is in business just as themselves. Another entity has been created to run the business, and this entity might over time acquire a monetary value.

Why might I set up as a Limited Company?

Broadly speaking, businesses decide to become Limited Companies instead of continuing as sole traders in order to get three advantages:

i. The *liability* of the owners is limited to the value of the company.

ii. A more professional appearance.

iii. The ability to accumulate value, and to accumulate funds at a lower rate of tax.

A special extra advantage applies to businesses producing theatre, dance or film/TV – special tax reliefs which are only available to Limited Companies – we discuss this more in the next chapter.

i. The liability of the owners is limited to the value of the company

This is the thing that is 'limited'; that's what 'limited' means. Why might this limitation be valuable? Here's a scenario that explains why people running businesses often want it.

Let's say that I open a pet shop called 'Jon's Pet Emporium', and I decide to remain a sole trader.

I begin stocking Rocket-Dog, a dog treat that I import from China, which is said to make dogs run faster.

Unfortunately, it turns out after some months that Rocket-Dog is poisonous, and all the dogs whose owners I have sold it to sadly fall sick (don't worry – they all recover fine after expensive vet treatments. No imaginary dogs were harmed in the publication of this book). Those owners now obviously have a legal claim against me, for the distress and medical costs that my actions have cost them.

Because I was a sole trader, the dog owners take legal action against me personally. I was trading as 'Jon's Pet Emporium', but I was still a sole trader, so the business and I were the same legal entity – and so the dog owners' claim is *against me personally*.

Suppose they are awarded £1m damages in court, and suppose I own a house (albeit with a mortgage) worth less than £1m. My house will be sold to pay the debt to them if I cannot pay in any other way. I will lose my house.

Now compare this to the same scenario, only this time assume that I am not a sole trader. I had instead decided, when the pet shop opened, to form a Limited Company called 'Jon's Pet Emporium Ltd', of which I was the only shareholder and Director.

This time, when the same Rocket-Dog disaster happens, the dog owners do not have a claim against me personally, but only against *the company*. My liability is limited to the assets and the value of the company, not my own assets. I will probably lose the business, because all its stock and equipment will be sold to go towards the debt. But I will not lose my house, my car or my TV, because I own these personally and the company does not.

This distinction also has an important bearing on my future activities. If I go bankrupt as a sole trader, apart from losing all my possessions and money, it will be relatively hard for me to start another business. The court will appoint someone to supervise me doing so, and that person may not agree to everything I want to do.

But if I lose my Limited Company in the same scenario, then provided I did not do anything illegal or negligent, I can start a new Limited Company tomorrow. (And I did not do anything negligent. I swear. Rocket-Dog had a string of good reviews which I checked before I started selling it. The whole thing was just bad luck.)

So, businesses tend to want to become Limited Companies because the risk they are taking in business is too great for them to want to bear on their own, as private individuals.

Very many creative freelancers – including the vast majority of performers – do not, in practice, take any or much risk at all in their business that may affect others. (An exception to this would be freelance dance teachers, yoga teachers, or stage combat instructors.) It's just not the nature of the game. This advantage is therefore likely to be of very minimal importance to performers.

Other types of creatives, though – for example, producers, or anybody making and selling products – may want to look out for these common milestones in the life of a business, which I usually advise create a reason to form a Limited Company, or at least to consider it very seriously:

- **Employing assistants or others on a PAYE payroll.** Technically, you can do this as a sole trader, but the risk involved in being an employer is significant and I would not really advise anyone to bear that risk as a private individual.

- **Leasing an office, studio or workshop.** Commercial leases tend to confer lots of responsibilities and liabilities, and here again I do not think it is sensible for most people to do that under their own personal banner.

- **Contracting with someone to do something where they will be in difficulty if you fail to deliver.** You can see immediately that this doesn't really apply to actors. If producers cast you and you drop out, they'll probably just get someone else and not have any difficulty in doing so. But if you contract to produce a show at a venue, or to deliver 5,000 framed photos to an art fair, you will cause the other party to the contract a big problem if you don't do it, and then they might sue you, and those are the circumstances where you want your liability to be limited.

ii. A more professional appearance

Many businesses choose to incorporate as Limited Companies because they believe that this confers a more professional appearance. They are hoping that customers, suppliers, funders and partners may be likely to view the business as more substantial if it is a Limited Company, and that therefore more people will want to do more, and more valuable, business with it.

Whether this is true or not depends on the sector you are in and the particular types of parties you are hoping to attract. If I want to get my hair cut, I am unlikely to choose Bob Scissors Ltd over Robert Scissors just because the former is a Limited Company and the latter is not. But if you want to sell mushroom pies to Tesco to stock on their shelves, you will find that they will only consider doing business with you if you are a Limited Company.

Probably only you can judge, based on your plans for your business and the types of people you are hoping to deal with, whether this is an advantage to you or not.

iii. The ability to accumulate funds at a lower rate of tax

We've arrived at a very tricky and complex issue.

It is almost certainly *not* true to say that Alex will pay less tax if they operate through a Limited Company, than if they operate as a sole trader.

But something else *is* true, that sounds a bit like the thing that is *not* true, hence the confusion. Let's unpick this.

Sole traders are taxed on *all* the profit they make, regardless of whether the business owner '*draws*' or takes that profit out of the bank, or not.

Limited Companies, by contrast, are only *fully* taxed on the profits that their owners draw out.

The only tax they pay on *all* their profit is Corporation Tax, which usually has a lower rate than income tax.

Suppose Alex begins to do very well and earns a lot of money in acting fees over the coming years; suppose they do several ads or movies or TV series, and suppose that their fee income in a year is now greatly exceeding what they need to live on. In those circumstances, there is a strong case for Alex to form a Limited Company. If they remained a sole trader, they would be taxed on all the profit they have made, regardless of whether they have taken it out of the bank to spend, left it there, or made other investments with it.

But if Alex is incorporated as Alex Actor Ltd, the position is different. The company is taxed at a *lower* rate on those profits, and then Alex personally only pays income tax on what they actually draw out of the bank and pay themselves. Alex does not pay tax on what is left, and could invest it in any number of ways without paying as much tax on it in the year in which it was earned.

They could also, at the point where their career plateaus, or even at the point of retirement, ultimately take that profit in the future at a lower rate of tax. (There used to be a very generously low tax rate in these circumstances, to 'encourage entrepreneurship'. In very recent years that benefit has been made much less generous, but it's still worth paying attention to.)

Right, so: Alex's dad's friend told Alex's dad in the pub that Alex should form a Limited Company because they will pay less tax if they do. Is this true?

Short answer – probably not.

Slightly longer answer – probably not, although as I said above, if they earn a lot of money over a long period it is more likely to be true.

Even longer answer – probably not, although if they earn a lot of money over a long period it is more likely to be true, and the Limited Company probably also represents a better way for Alex to arrange their long-term pension provision as an alternative to paying into a personal pension scheme.

It's beyond the scope of this book to get into all the reasons behind these rules-of-thumb. The important thing for Alex to remember is that they can ignore the common urban myth, that 'you should form a Limited Company because you pay less tax', at least until they start to earn considerably more than, say, £100,000 per year for several years in a row.

One of the reasons that Alex's dad's friend holds the view that he does is because he has heard of a payment method called dividends.

A Limited Company can pay its Directors as PAYE employees, and can also pay its shareholders dividends. This simply means a share of the profits. There are some circumstances in which dividend tax (a form of income tax payable through a person's self-assessment return) might work out less than income tax on work earnings. Alex's dad's friend has taken this kernel of truth and blown it up into an oak-tree of nonsense: most sole-shareholder-Directors of one-person Limited Companies receiving dividends will in fact pay the same amount of income tax as if they had run the business as sole traders.

I do not usually make a habit of maligning my fellow accountants, but one of the reasons why this urban myth has such a powerful hold is that some unscrupulous accountants promote it because they charge higher fees for Limited Company clients than for sole trader clients. So be careful whose advice you listen to on this point and, at risk of repetition, the advice of a specialist accountant will be better than the advice listened to in the pub and even that of non-specialist accountants.

Incidentally, an additional aspect of this motivation for forming a Limited Company is that in doing so, it is easier to create a business which has a saleable value, if one day you want to leave it and sell it to someone else.

Sole traders tend not to sell their businesses: they retire, or stop and do something else. And if Alex forms Alex Actor Ltd, they will also probably never sell it: it only has a meaning to Alex themselves. But if you are thinking of forming a production company, or opening a camera shop, you may well have something to sell when the day comes that you want to stop, and this is more easily done as a Limited Company.

How do Limited Companies report and pay their tax?

Inherent in the answer to this question are some of the disadvantages to operating Limited Companies: basically, they cost more money, more time and more effort to operate.

As we have seen so far in this book, if Alex starts in business as a sole trader, they will essentially have only one legal obligation every year: to compile and file a tax return from their records.

But if Alex forms Alex Actor Ltd, the company will have *four* annual obligations, in addition to the more involved paperwork required to start (and eventually to stop) the company:

i. A Limited Company files its accounts every year at Companies House.

ii. It also files a Corporation Tax return every year, and pays any tax due.

iii. It files an annual Confirmation Statement at Companies House – this is a legal document that confirms various details about the company and the fact that it still exists.

iv. Alex will almost certainly still need to do a self-assessment return as well, and this has become a slightly more complex exercise than the one we looked at earlier because it now needs to take account of the relationship between Alex and the company. Alex has earned their own personal income for the year by taking a mixture of a PAYE salary from the company, and flexible dividends, and maybe still PAYE from other employers too. Accounting for all this can get complicated.

This all adds up to extra costs for Alex, probably in accountancy fees. In Chapter 2, we discussed whether sole-trader Alex would need an accountant to compile his self-assessment return or not. We concluded that some people will want to use an accountant, but that many will not need to. This is not true for the owners of Limited Companies. Limited Company accounts and Corporation Tax returns are not documents that a non-professional can correctly compile by themselves (although I've seen a lot of people try, and come unstuck).

Another batch of disadvantages to operating a Limited Company come about because of the increased visibility and reduced confidentiality that is required if you operate in this way. This is completely logical, right? If you want me to contract with you as a Limited Company – that's to say, you want me to risk that if you don't deliver on what you have promised to, I will only have limited recourse to get my money back – then it is only fair that you should have to tell me more about yourself.

Therefore these basic facts about a Limited Company are much more public than the same facts about a sole trader:

- **The company's address.** This is instantly searchable online for free, as are the names and addresses of the Directors. It is often possible to use a more anonymous address, say, for example, your accountants' office, or a commercial PO Box-type address where a service provider will receive your mail and forward it to you, but of course there is a cost for these services.

- **The company's accounts.** These are also instantly searchable online for free. Until now, most small companies have not been required to publicise their Profit and Loss statement – the page of the accounts that shows clearly how much money the company earned and how much it spent in the year. But the regime in the UK on this point is changing, and within a couple of years of the time of writing, you will need to publicise this. So Alex needs to recognise that if they form a Limited Company, anyone at all will be able to see how much they have earned in any year.

If you are a sole trader, nobody can search for these details. The only people apart from you who know how much money you are making are HMRC. You also do not need to do any ID check with HMRC when you start. But in 2025, Companies House also introduced a rigorous regime of ID checks for Limited Company Directors, adding to the considerable number of hurdles Alex is going to need to jump if they want to trade as Alex Actor Ltd.

VAT disaggregation

Sometimes sole traders do not want to cross the VAT threshold of £90,000 in any twelve months because they do not want to charge VAT. Remember Alex and those guitar lessons (see page 177)? He wanted to save VAT on agent commission, but did not want to start charging VAT on guitar lessons. Sometimes those in this position make an error in their tax strategy because they do not know about the concept of VAT disaggregation.

> Let's consider the case of Imogen, a writer and yoga teacher. Imogen has had a couple of very decent years in both her trades. She has earned about £50,000 in each of the past two years from writing. Her yoga activities got off to a slower start, but now she has established some successful groups, and also established a few long-term relationships with clients who pay a high hourly rate for her to do yoga sessions with them at their homes.
>
> Imogen considers VAT registration for two reasons:
>
> i. She will be *obliged* to register, remember, if she hits a £90,000 threshold overall in any twelve-month period.
>
> ii. She is billing her writing work through her agent, and therefore heeds the advice I gave on page 178, that with that level of income, voluntary VAT registration is likely to save her money.
>
> However, Imogen is disinclined to register for VAT in her particular case, because if she does, she will need to start charging VAT to her yoga customers, all of whom are, of course, private individuals and cannot therefore reclaim VAT. Imogen is facing the same dilemma Alex faced: let's review it from her perspective. Say Imogen charges

£20 for attendance at a yoga class. If she becomes VAT-registered she will need to do one of three unhappy things:

i. Put her price up to £20 + VAT = £24. Painful for her customers, but not for her (a bit like the yoga class itself?), though it also presumably risks her overpricing and losing customers.

ii. Suffer the VAT herself, and only keep £20/1.2 = £16.67 herself instead of the full £20.

iii. A halfway house – maybe put the price up to £22, and take £18.33. Half the pain for her, and half for her customer.

'Ah-HA,' thinks Imogen. 'So I know what I'll do, to avoid any of these three! I'll form a Limited Company for the yoga, called Imogen's Yoga Ltd. I'll continue as a sole trader for my writing work, and I'll use the Limited Company for all my yoga work. That way, the £90,000 threshold will be split between the two separate entities, and I can do both without VAT. Or even better, I can register as a sole trader for VAT on writing work, and claim back the VAT on my agent commission, without also having to collect VAT on yoga lessons!'

Nice try, Imogen. Unfortunately this wheeze will not work because of the VAT disaggregation rules.

VAT legislation is the only sort of legislation that *looks through* the legal distinction between companies and individuals. So, in VAT terms, Imogen's sole tradership and her Limited Company are one and the same, even though they file their accounts and tax returns differently.

So this means there is no way round Imogen grappling with one or other of the imperfect choices described above.

If this feels unfair to you, consider what would happen if this rule were not in place. Every pub would be run by five different companies, one selling beer, one selling wine, one main courses and so on; Marks & Spencer's would form 10,000 different companies, all of them selling different types of clothing. And then the government would never collect any VAT, and all public services would collapse (DON'T SAY IT).

Partnerships

Finally, let's consider Partnerships, which are a kind of halfway house between sole traders and Limited Companies.

A Partnership is formed when two or more people start trading in a business together. It is neatest and most sensible for a Partnership to be registered with HMRC, but that is not actually *necessary* to create a legal Partnership.

Some care is needed here, because it is easy to 'fall into' a legal Partnership without intending to and without thinking through the implications.

Suppose Imogen has now become too busy to personally take the yoga class she started at Springfield Village Hall on Tuesday evenings. So she discusses the situation with her friend Melanie, another freelance yoga teacher. They agree verbally that Imogen will continue to market and take bookings for the class, but Melanie will actually teach it. Attenders will continue to pay Imogen, and Imogen will give Melanie 75% of the takings.

It could be argued that this situation might have created an employer-employee relationship between Imogen and Melanie, but I do not think it has (a complicated question in itself).

If Imogen and Melanie leave their agreement there, I believe that a de facto Partnership has been created. It is reasonable to suppose that the attenders of the class might look at Imogen and Melanie and presume that it is a Partnership, because they know that it is not a Limited Company (it doesn't say 'limited' on the booking confirmation they are given) and it seems reasonable to assume that Melanie is not Imogen's employee. And a Partnership is, like beauty, in the eye of the beholder.

Now say that one of the attenders thinks they have a claim against the class; say, for example, that they tripped over some equipment and sustained an injury. This person is entitled to claim that Imogen and Melanie have a Partnership *simply because it appears that they do*. It does not matter that Imogen and Melanie didn't sign a Partnership agreement.

This means that if Imogen was hoping to duck any responsibility for the incident because it was Melanie's class, or if Melanie is hoping to do so because it was Imogen's hall booking, they are both wrong. They are Partners, and they will both be liable if the attender's claim against them is successful.

It would have been more sensible for Imogen and Melanie to establish a Partnership formally at the outset, and set out in detail in a Partnership agreement:

- Who would be doing what.

- Who would be putting in any money upfront to meet the Partnership's expenses.

- How the income would be split – what percentage each Partner's share is.

- What liabilities each Partner has to the other Partners, to the customers, suppliers, etc.

The Partnership should then be registered with HMRC and receive its own UTR (Unique Tax Reference number).

The Partnership needs to have its own bank account and keep records of its income and expenses, including receipts for expenses, just like any other kind of business.

At the end of the tax year, the Partnership makes up its accounts so that each Partner can see what their share of the profit (or loss) is.

Say that Imogen and Melanie agreed that the Partnership income would first have expenses deducted from it, such as hall hire costs, marketing and admin costs. Then the remaining profit would be split 75:25 in Melanie's favour.

Say that at the end of the 2025/26 year, there is profit of £2,000, so Melanie takes £1,500 and Imogen takes £500.

The Partnership submits its own tax return to HMRC, but it does not pay any tax directly. Instead, Melanie adds the £1,500 to a special Partnership section of her self-assessment tax return, and adds it to any other income she had during the year to calculate her personal tax bill, and, of course, Imogen does the same with her £500.

Thus, if you are a Partner in a Partnership that makes its own tax return, this job needs to have been finished before you can finish your self-assessment return, otherwise you will not know what to write in the Partnership section.

Some advantages of operating a Partnership instead of a Limited Company in the creative industries are:

- It's much easier to open it and close it.
- Fewer reporting requirements, none of them public.

- It confers some of the 'professional appearance' benefit that accrues to Limited Companies – it looks more established than a sole tradership.

But there are disadvantages: a Partnership does not have limited liability, and also will not qualify for Theatre or Film Tax Relief, which is very important to theatre and film producers, and which we will look at in more detail in the next chapter.

Golden rules for Limited Companies

- It's probably of no real *tax* benefit to you, but there may be other benefits.

- Take professional advice before you incorporate a Limited Company.

- Splitting your business using a Limited Company is not a way to avoid the VAT threshold.

- Beware the danger of falling into a Partnership without setting it up properly first.

7. Producing Your Own Work

So far, we have mostly discussed the business activities of sole trader freelancers whose main goal, like Alex, is to sell the personal work of their own brain, body and soul to a producer of, say, a theatre or film production. The producer already has the vehicle, and Alex's aim is to be invited to ride in and help operate it.

This chapter is a short introduction to some of the financial aspects and practicalities of putting on your own theatre or film productions as a first-time or small producer, or establishing a business that sells products or services to a larger number of customers, without the support of a larger company, under your own auspices. You could think of this as building your own vehicle, into which you will invite others, to help you operate it.

Producing your own work is a complex undertaking, and this is only a short and simple chapter. There are whole books and indeed degree courses out there that teach all the skills necessary for this, and I am not hoping to summarise or replicate these in this chapter.

It is clear, however, that many freelancers in Alex's position turn their thoughts to producing their own work, so I want to analyse these thoughts to some degree, and offer some starting points and ideas for further reflection, through the lens of finance and taxation, which should assist Alex in this process.

Why is self-producing common?

We discussed in Chapter 1 some possible ways of supplementing income from fees that you earn when being hired for creative work. We observed that you are very likely to need to supplement income in this way, especially in the early years of your career. We discussed that self-producing is one of the options, provided you can find a way to make it pay. Here are some of the reasons why it is often one of the best options:

- Self-producing is something you decide to do for yourself: you are not dependent on anyone else inviting you or allowing you to do it. You can simply have an idea and set about implementing it.

- It is likely to be more fun than the other options.

- When you are self-producing, you are creating a shop window for the very creative skills that you are trained in, and that you want to concentrate on. If you are working at a 'job in a pub', or in another field entirely, you are obviously not doing so: there is really only a financial motive for spending time in that way.

- It is possible to persuade donors or investors to support your self-produced work, whereas they are much less likely to donate to or invest in your attempt to get hired as a creative in someone else's work.

- It is possible to apply to Arts Council England to support projects that fall within its remit. Before the pandemic, it was very rare for the Arts Council to support small-scale projects run by individual creatives, but now it has become much more common. (Beware, though – it's relatively easy to apply for this funding, but I'm not saying it's easy to be awarded it. It's very competitive.)

- If you want to produce theatre or film, the State supports this modestly through tax reliefs (more on this later).

- Many self-producers are pleasantly surprised to find that they have underestimated the demand for the service they have in mind, and that it is easier than they thought to market and sell it. Here are a few examples:

> **Ashley** noticed that her local pub did not have a weekly comedy night. So she spoke to the manager, did a deal, and began promoting one. She found it relatively easy to start booking acts, hosting open-mic nights and selling tickets, often simply to friends and friends of friends.
>
> Remember **Imogen** from Chapter 6 and her expanding network of yoga classes.
>
> **Nitin** has circus and magic skills, and he found it quite easy to market his children's birthday parties using local networks.
>
> **Katherine** had an idea for making a particular style of scented candle. By careful research about purchasing materials to make the candles very cheaply, she was able to start selling them at a local market and online at a huge mark-up.

Can I self-produce as a sole trader, or do I need to start a Limited Company?

In Chapter 6 (from page 185) we looked at the concept of Limited Companies, and we considered whether Alex should or should not incorporate a Limited Company for their sole trader business as an actor. Our conclusion was probably not for the time being, because it is likely that none of the three main benefits of Limited Companies apply to Alex's activities as a performer – that is to say:

i. They aren't taking any financial risks; they won't owe anyone else anything if things go wrong.

ii. They don't operate in an industry where Limited Company actors are considered to be more professional than sole trader ones, like some other industries.

iii. There isn't a tax advantage unless or until Alex starts to make a lot more money over a long period.

These three judgements may well *not* be the same if we now consider Alex's business as a self-producing one, instead of simply a trying-to-get-hired one. Let's say that Alex has written a play, *Murder at the Tax Office*, and is considering forming a theatre company to produce it. Now Alex's judgement on the three main reasons for forming a Limited Company may well be the opposite:

i. A contract with a venue to put on a play creates financial responsibilities and liabilities. If something goes wrong, Alex might end up owing the venue a lot of money.

ii. Some venues and suppliers prefer to deal with Limited Companies.

iii. Crucially, Alex's play will qualify for Theatre Tax Relief if produced by a Limited Company, but it will not do so if produced by Alex as a sole trader.

So now the argument for forming a Limited Company is more compelling. It is interesting to apply these arguments to the examples we looked at above. We notice that each case is different:

> **Ashley** probably has only a very small liability to the pub hosting the comedy night, even if something goes wrong. It's only once a week, for small rent. She probably does not need the professional appearance of a Limited Company, and stand-up comedy is not eligible for Theatre Tax Relief. Verdict: don't form a Limited Company.
>
> **Imogen** may be facing mounting liabilities. Inherent in physical activity is the risk of injury to customers. As Imogen builds her network of classes, so her risks grow. Verdict: seriously consider a Limited Company.
>
> **Nitin** needs to think quite carefully about the liability issue. Selling services to children may inherently bring more liability and more process. For example, Nitin should ensure that all those he engages to help work with him are DBS-checked, and he may simply feel more comfortable protecting himself more against possible difficulties. Verdict: consider a Limited Company.
>
> **Katherine** isn't taking much risk if her activities remain at a reasonably small scale, and if her suppliers are happy to contract with her as an individual. But if the candle business grows, and needs to order more stock, or take on employees, or rent premises, or sell wholesale to shops which will sell the candles on, then these will be milestones that probably need a Limited Company. Verdict: one to watch.

So, think carefully about your particular activity and your ambitions. Remember also that the decision about whether to incorporate is not a one-time decision: you can keep reviewing it.

Different structures of producing businesses

Now let's summarise the different types of producing businesses and consider what type of Limited Company you need if you decide to incorporate – because there are several types.

- **Sole trader** – basically what this book has been about so far, per the definition at the start of Chapter 2.

- **Partnership.** We met this beast in Chapter 6. Bear in mind that if you get together with associates, like Imogen working with Melanie on the yoga classes, and you do not form a Limited Company, then outside parties, or HMRC, might come along and tell you that you have a de facto Partnership, even if you have not yourself formally established one. There is more about this from page 199.

- **Private company limited by shares.** This is the type of Limited Company we have been thinking about so far. This is the company I advise Alex to form in order to produce theatre productions, and that I advise Katherine to form once she takes on her first candle-making employee, or reaches one of the other watersheds suggested. This is a company with (probably) its main guiding persona being the only shareholder and Director. There is only one share, and you own it yourself.

- **Private company limited by guarantee.** This is the same as a share company except in one respect: instead of having shares and shareholders, the company has a guarantee and members. This means that rather than the shareholders risking the value of their shares in the activities of the business, the members risk the amount they have said they will guarantee – usually a nominal sum of £1.

Thus a guarantee company confers all the same benefits of limited liability and professional appearance as a share company. The only difference is that it cannot distribute profits, and it does not have shares which can increase in value like Google's shares can – the company itself can never be worth a specific value, like a share company can.

Doing business as a guarantee company is a quick shorthand way of telling the world that your business is a not-for-profit business. Those who work for it (including you) can be paid a normal market rate for their work, but will not be paid dividends, as in a share company. So forming a guarantee company can be a quick and efficient way of telling certain kinds of funders that you are a not-for-profit; if, for example, you are doing work which is for public benefit and you think you may be able to raise money from charitable trusts and foundations. Some care is needed here. Some funders have more detailed requirements than others, and simply forming a guarantee company is only a shorthand. To be eligible for more and different types of funding, a guarantee company might need to add clauses to its constitution, or write additional policies, shoring up its not-for-profit intentions.

- **Community Interest Company (CIC).** CIC status can be given either to a company limited by shares or limited by guarantee (although in the creative industries CICs limited by guarantee are much more normal), and creates an additional set of circumstances. Operating a CIC also signals to funders and to the public that your activities are for public benefit. A CIC does this more visibly than a guarantee company. Firstly, more people know and understand that 'CIC' means 'for public benefit' than understand this same thing about a 'private company limited by guarantee'. Secondly, a CIC has to make a public report every year, detailing what it has done to help the community.

There is more paperwork involved in incorporating and running a CIC, but some creative businesses accept this extra work because they find that the more public 'badge' of a CIC assists them in fundraising efforts.

- **Public Limited Company (PLC).** This a very large company, like Tesco or Google, whose shares can be bought by any member of the public on a stock exchange.

- **Registered Charity.** Operating a charity confers two very large advantages to creative businesses. Firstly, it is obviously much easier to attract donations from the public, and grants from foundations and many other types of funders, if you are a charity. Secondly, a charity can make as much profit as it likes, entirely tax-free. No other type of company can do this, not even a CIC.

A charity *can* simultaneously be a company limited by guarantee, but it does not need to be – it can be a Charitable Incorporated Organisation (CIO), which is a registered business in its own right limiting the liability of the Trustees.

Obviously, much greater restrictions accompany these advantages. A charity is regulated by the Charity Commission, much more strictly and onerously than other kinds of companies. The Charity Commission can make all kinds of detailed demands about the way the organisation operates, and generally require considerable amounts of paperwork both when the charity is first established, and as it continues. A charity must be run by at least three Trustees and they cannot receive any financial benefit from their involvement (although there are circumstances where they could be paid normal market rates for working for the charity – but even that is complicated).

In practice, this means that running a charity is a different concept to running your own company, from the perspective of an individual creative entrepreneur. A charity is a bigger thing, so to speak; it must be clear how it is contributing to public benefit. It can't be simply a vehicle for one person's work, which all the other structures can be and often are.

Deciding which type of company to form can be a very complex choice, on which you may need to take advice from a specialist accountant or solicitor. There are also some very good independent consultants out there who help small creative organisations with this choice. Let's take a look at our examples and see if we can come to any conclusions...

Alex's theatre production company. Alex should make this choice depending on the type of work they are producing and their realistic ambitions for its future. Are they trying to form a broadly commercial enterprise, which might one day make some proper commercial profit and build value? Or are they aiming to produce work which is less commercial in nature, and which is likely always to need subsidy or donations to support it? And will it be possible to get that subsidy? The former would lead me to advise forming a limited share company, while the latter would lead me to advise forming a guarantee company, which should perhaps also be a CIC, and which may have ambitions to become a registered charity in the longer term.

Imogen's yoga company. Imogen could choose to formalise a Partnership with Melanie. But if her ambition is to grow her network of classes, and bearing in mind the potential risk of injury to customers, I tend to advise her to form a limited share company.

Nitin's children's parties. Unless Nitin plans a type of party, or future activities, which are for community benefit – perhaps he envisages offering subsidised parties to those who need them, or expanding his activities to offer subsidised circus-skills classes – he should either continue as a sole trader, or incorporate a share company. More subsidised or educational activities might lead him towards a guarantee company and a CIC.

Katherine's candles. Katherine is a classic case for a share company, once she reaches one of the growth milestones we discussed earlier.

Creative Industry Tax Reliefs

I have mentioned a few times that Creative Industry Tax Reliefs – Theatre Tax Relief (TTR) and Film Tax Relief (FTR) – represent one of the main benefits of incorporating a company if you want to produce theatre or film. Let's have a look at what these reliefs actually are, and consider some of the pros and cons of trying to get them.

For some years, successive governments have tried to create a tax regime to support theatre and film production which does something to re-establish the higher levels of subsidy that existed before, but which doesn't cost governments so much money. Out of this ambition were born these reliefs.

We could debate all day whether this is a good thing or not, but I think it is fair to judge that this system will be with us for a good while yet, and so the creative sector industry bodies have tended to welcome it and to encourage both government commitment to it, and industry take-up of the support provided.

In general terms, TTR and FTR give financial support to Limited Companies producing theatre shows and films, which pass certain tests of eligibility (we'll consider these in more detail below, but they are not very onerous tests).

Imagine you have gone through the process of setting up a Limited Company in order to produce theatre shows and films. Support in the form of tax relief is given via the company's corporation tax return process:

i. If the company has made a profit, the TTR or FTR allows it to reduce the amount of corporation tax payable.

ii. If the company has made a loss, the TTR or FTR allows it to claim a certain sum from HMRC, equivalent to the amount that the tax bill *would* have been reduced by if the company had been in profit.

The value of the claim is a certain percentage of the 'production costs' or 'core costs' (more on what that means below) of the show or film. The exact percentage varies quite a bit depending on various circumstances, but a rule of thumb is that a producing company can expect to claim about a third of the core costs of making a show, and about a quarter of the core costs of making a film.

Some of the advantages of the TTR and FTR system are that:

- If you qualify, the money is yours by right. TTR and FTR are legal entitlements to money. They are not given 'at the discretion' of HMRC, in the way that grants are given at the discretion of funding bodies like the Arts Council. In one important way this makes your activities easier to plan, since you can be certain from your planning stage that, provided you follow all the rules, the money will definitely come.

- The timing of you receiving the money is also (to within a few weeks, in the majority of cases) completely predictable. This is obviously not the case if you embark on a fundraising or donation campaign, which will take as long as it takes.

In practice, these are such huge advantages to a small producer that I tend to advise that nobody should nowadays produce an eligible production as a sole trader or Partnership, because that will not be eligible for TTR/FTR. If your production is eligible, you are almost certain to earn more money from it if you produce it as a Limited Company and therefore qualify for TTR/FTR, even despite the higher costs of forming and operating a Limited Company.

Some of the disadvantages of the scheme are:

- Its rules are hopelessly, ridiculously, risibly arbitrary. For example: a loaf of bread that you buy as a prop for the dress rehearsal is an eligible 'core cost', but the same loaf of bread you buy for the tenth performance is not. Go figure.

- Because it is a tax relief system and not a grant system, its technicalities are extremely hard to follow if you are not a fully qualified and probably industry-specialist accountant. I am aware that there are theatre and film producers who do try to complete their own tax returns and TTR/FTR claims. I have never seen a DIY one without several mistakes in it.

- The money is only paid to you some months after the completion of your project, unlike grant money or donated money which is generally paid to you in advance of your project. So in cashflow terms, you have to be able to pay all the project bills and survive, while you are waiting for the money to arrive.

Now let's look at some of the nuts and bolts of the scheme and consider the various hoops you need to jump through in order to be sure that you will qualify for the support.

The production must be of a certain type

Theatre: the legislation tries to allow all 'standard' plays to qualify, while trying to disallow genres like stand-up comedy, shows of a sexual nature in nightclubs (NB. The particular paragraph of the legislation that describes this is utterly hilarious), circus shows, and talent shows. Many shows very obviously qualify, but this area does get a bit difficult around shows that play with the boundary between fiction and reality, or which have audience participation, such as immersive theatre – you may well need specialist advice if you produce that type of work.

Dance: the legislation rather quaintly uses the word 'ballet' to describe what kinds of dance shows qualify. This is a very broad use of the word. The vast majority of shows that we would describe as 'contemporary dance' do qualify, because they tend to be founded in choreography that derives at least in part from classical ballet techniques.

You may be in trouble if your performers simply walk on stage and wiggle their shoulders a bit.

Film: the film constraints are tighter. The film has to be 'British', and the legislation offers some very tight definitions of what that means, and how the film qualifies. The BFI is the final arbiter of what is and isn't 'British', and every film needs to be signed off with a certificate from the BFI in order to qualify. This creates another layer of bureaucracy for FTR which does not exist for TTR.

There must be either a commercial purpose ('separately ticketed') or an educational purpose

A significant proportion of the live performances of a show must be ticketed events to qualify. There must also either be a genuine commercial attempt to sell tickets to the public, or an obvious educational purpose (e.g. the performances take place in schools or colleges). The legislation excludes events that are not 'separate', so, for example, an outdoor show happening as part of a festival will not qualify, even if the audience had to pay to be admitted to the festival.

The Limited Company must pay all the bills

Sometimes small-scale producers wise up to the importance of Theatre Tax Relief after they have already produced the show as a sole trader, and then try retrospectively to incorporate a company and pass the production to it. This will not wash. The Limited Company making the claim has to be the business that did the producing at the time.

Core costs must be distinguished from non-core costs

This is the hardest part of the TTR and FTR system to understand. Only some of the production costs are eligible and not others. The legislation makes an attempt to draw a distinction between 'core' costs – i.e. costs that were incurred in the *creation* of the work – and 'non-core' costs, being costs that were incurred in the *operation* of the work.

Please do not write to me and ask why this is so. It is a completely arbitrary and meaningless distinction. It gives rise to a host of fiddly rules about which costs can be claimed and which cannot (remember those two identical loaves of bread on page 214). But we are stuck with this system and that is that. If you are producing your own work and can benefit from TTR/FTR, don't waste your time trying to understand this – just follow the rules that have been laid out.

To help understand this, consider that a company is likely to have three phases of creating a work:

i. Development – it is thinking about a project that it hasn't committed to yet.

ii. Production – it commits to the project and creates it, ready to present/release it.

iii. Presentation/Release – the work is out there being consumed by its audience.

TTR/FTR-eligible costs are, broadly speaking, the costs that belong in the second of these phases, the production phase, and not the other two.

For a **theatre show**, this is likely to mean that budget lines such as the creative team fees; the rehearsal costs;

and the physical production costs like sets, costumes and props form the bulk of eligible costs in a claim.

For a film, it is likely to mean that budget lines such as the creative team fees; rehearsal and shooting costs; physical production costs like sets, costumes, props, electrics and camera hires; and post-production facility costs form the bulk of eligible costs in a claim.

Marketing costs are specifically excluded.

Obviously, the foundation of a smooth claim is good book-keeping. Your accountant is going to need to submit a very detailed form to HMRC stating all your eligible costs; and therefore you save a lot of time, cost and trouble if you annotate or tag your expenditure in whatever software or spreadsheet you are using to record it, as you go along. Otherwise it can be quite difficult to unpick which costs are eligible and which costs are not.

> Remember that Alex Actor Ltd is producing *Murder in the Tax Office*. Alex has hired Waleed, an actor, to play the part of Mr Smith, a tax inspector. Waleed's fee is £500 per week and he invoices Alex Actor Ltd weekly. In the first week of October, the show is in tech on Monday, Tuesday and Wednesday. It opens on Thursday and plays to Saturday. This means that half of Waleed's invoice for that week is an eligible cost to Alex Actor Ltd, because it relates to 'production costs', and half is not, because it relates to 'presentation'. So you can see that in order to be able to make a correct claim without going completely berserk, Alex Actor Ltd will need an effective, detailed, well-thought-through book-keeping system that identifies the eligible costs.

Costs must be spent in the UK

Eligible costs are those that have been spent in the UK, or, if they have been spent overseas (for example, if a set has been built overseas), the benefit has only been realised in the UK (i.e. the set was not actually used in any shows overseas).

All costs incurred in Europe used to be eligible. Now it's only the UK. Guess which way I voted in the Brexit referendum.

This section has given you only a short introduction to these tax reliefs. They are, as you can see, quite hard to get your head round. But they are undoubtedly a useful fundraising tool for you, and remember that professional help is always available to you at considerably less cost than the amounts you should be able to claim – so don't hesitate to use it.

VAT for producers

Finally, a few words on VAT for those making their own work.

In Chapter 6, we considered the VAT position as it relates to individual, sole trader creatives. The equation needs looking at again as soon as you are planning your own productions or commercial activities.

In much the same way as we discussed before, if your business is making sales of at least £90,000 in any twelve-month period, you do not have any choice about VAT – you have to register.

If you are making sales of lower than that threshold, however, you have a choice whether to register or not.

The issue of VAT on ticket sales for small-scale theatre producers is exceptionally complex and widely misunderstood. Let's consider this pitfall briefly, but I cannot overstate the importance of taking expert professional advice on this if it applies to you.

The problem arises because it is normal for a small-scale theatre producer to present their production in a venue which somebody else owns or controls. That should be obvious. Alex cannot present *Murder in the Tax Office* in their flat. They need to make a deal with a venue.

That deal may take one of several different forms. Alex might pay to hire the venue, or the venue might pay Alex a fee for the show and take the ticket money itself, or there might be an agreement to split the box-office takings in some proportion between Alex and the venue.

The venue may or may not be VAT-registered. All these ifs, buts and possibilities create a difficult and ever-changing playing-field around the issue of VAT on tickets, which might significantly affect Alex's financial position; so it is vital that this matter is considered, and a strategy understood and agreed on, at the point where the deal between Alex and the venue is being negotiated. Unfortunately, this matter is overlooked all too often, which is not to anyone's benefit. So get clear on this, and don't hesitate to take well-qualified expert advice on it.

Golden rules for producing your own work

- Don't be scared. This route is often a very useful and rewarding one.

- Carefully consider what the best business structure is for you, before you start.

- There is no one answer to this for everyone.
- Take professional advice if you need it.
- If you aren't making your work eligible for tax reliefs, why aren't you?
- Consider VAT again as a self-producer.

Appendices

Alex's career finance checklist

This checklist can be downloaded and personalised with your own relevant dates from: www.nickhernbooks.co.uk/money-resources.

Date	Task
July 2025	Graduate from course.
August 2025	Move to London flat and start work.
August 2025	Write a budget. Review it monthly.
August 2025	Register online with HMRC as self-employed using form SA1 (actually the deadline for this is much later – it is September 2026 – but I recommend that Alex gets out ahead of this deadline).
August 2025	Decide on a record-keeping system – probably easiest to go for an app from the beginning, or at the very least a Making Tax Digital-compliant spreadsheet. Keep it up to date, at least weekly.

August 2025 to March 2026	• Weekly book-keeping. Monthly budget review. • Save between 8% and 20% of untaxed earnings for eventual tax bill. • Think about private pension contributions, and savings.
March 2026	Decide whether to engage an accountant or to go it alone.
April & May 2026	Chase any missing bits of info about the 2025/26 year, e.g. P45s and P60s from PAYE jobs, interest certificates from banks.
May to July 2026	Best time to complete 2025/26 tax return (although the deadline is 31 Jan 2027).
July 2026	Submit first quarterly update (QU) under Making Tax Digital (voluntary in Alex's first year). This may not be mandatory for Alex until July 2027 or July 2028, or possibly not even then depending on Alex's income.
Summer 2026	Time to consider: i) is VAT registration necessary, or desirable? ii) is there any case for forming a Limited Company?
October 2026	Submit second QU.
January 2027	Submit third QU.
31 January 2027	Pay any tax that is due for 2025/26, plus the first part of 'payment on account', depending on level of earnings.
April 2027	Submit fourth QU.

April to May 2027	Chase any missing bits of info about the 2026/27 year, e.g. P45s and P60s from PAYE jobs, interest certificates from banks.
May to July 2027	Best time to complete 2026/27 tax return (although the deadline is 31 Jan 2028).
July 2027	Submit first quarterly update (QU) under Making Tax Digital *IF told to do so by HMRC – this depends on earnings level.* This still may not start for Alex until July 2028.
31 July 2027	Pay second payment on account. This is either the amount that was set by the 2025/26 return, or it might have been *reduced* by the 2026/27 return. Check that National Insurance Full Years are being correctly marked up on gov.uk.
Summer 2027	Time to consider: i) is VAT registration necessary, or desirable? ii) is there any case for forming a Limited Company?
October 2027	Submit second QU.
January 2028	Submit third QU.
31 January 2028	Pay any tax due for 2026/7 that was not covered by earlier payments on account, plus the first part of the new payment on account, depending on level of earnings.
April 2028	Submit fourth QU.
And so on until...	...
...2080	Retire. Party. Spain.

Glossary

Accountant – A person more useful than a solicitor, but sometimes not with as good a sense of humour.

Accrual accounting – Also called 'traditional' accounting. A method of preparing your accounts by 'recognising' your income and expenses, in effect counting them, at a time other than the time at which money actually changed hands; as opposed to cash accounting (which means counting items when you actually receive or pay the money for them).

Allowable – Also called 'deductible'. An expense that can correctly be deducted from income, thus reducing taxable profit.

At source – Usually, when someone paying you (like an employer, a bank, or a government department) deducts tax before they give you the money.

Capital – Depends on the context, but perhaps most helpfully 'a chunk of money that isn't income or expenditure, but is owned and earmarked or defined in some way'.

Capital Gains – The 'profit' made on an individual selling something valuable, e.g. property, valuable goods, crypto, or company shares. This type of profit is a gain, not income, and is taxed in a different way.

Capitalise – (Of a business, especially a new one) To gather funds to spend on new business, either by borrowing, by raising investment or by selling a less risky product or service in order to fund a riskier one.

Cash accounting – The opposite of accrual or 'traditional' accounting – dating and counting account items when you actually receive or pay them.

Directors – The people who run a Limited Company and are responsible for what it does. Not to be confused with the people who sit at the front of a rehearsal room drinking champagne while the actors do all the work.

Dividend – Money which a Limited Company pays to its shareholders to represent their share of profits it has made.

Earth – Mostly harmless.

Equity – The net value of something, most often in this context the amount of value in your property that you actually own, as opposed to any part which is mortgaged. (Also, confusingly, the trade union representing actors, because of a wholly different sense in which 'equity' means 'justice' or 'fairness'.)

Foreign Tax Credit – A mechanism by which, if you have had income tax deducted from an overseas fee before you received the fee, you don't have to pay tax on that income again in the UK.

Freelance – Self-employed.

Government Gateway – A portal where you have an account with the State, for functions such as tax and NI.

Gross (and net) – These terms can be confusing and dependent on context, but they usually mean 'including everything' (gross) and 'with some bits taken out' (net). For example:

- In a conversation about your self-employment income for the year, 'gross' means 'before you take the expenses off' and 'net' means after you do.

- In a conversation about VAT, 'gross' means the sum the customer pays including VAT, and 'net' means the sum after taking the VAT off.

- In a conversation about a fee paid for acting work via an agent, 'gross' means the actor's full fee as paid by the employer, and 'net' means the amount after agent commission is taken off.

- In a conversation about box-office takings in a theatre, 'gross' means the total box-office sales, and 'net' means the sales after deducting VAT, credit-card commission, ticket fees, and possibly royalties too.

I said it was confusing.

Incorporate – To form a Limited Company.

Interest – Usually, money which A pays B because B lent A some money, or B gave A some money to look after.

Invoice – Another word for 'bill'. A self-employed person sends this to whoever engaged them to do the work, in exactly the same way as a waiter hands you the restaurant bill at the end of the meal.

IR35 – HMRC-speak for a type of working arrangement where people who should be treated as employed are instead treated as self-employed. Now largely irrelevant in the arts except insofar as it relates to star names earning very large sums from one broadcaster.

Limited Company – A business which is legally separate from the humans who own and control it.

Making Tax Digital – HMRC's system, introduced in the 2020s, for more frequent and more detailed reporting of self-assessment matters than was the case before.

Members – The equivalent of the shareholders in a company limited by guarantee – they are like the owners, only there's nothing to own.

Mortgage – A loan, often large and long-term, lent to someone to buy a property with. 'Mortgaged': a property which has a mortgage outstanding on it.

National Insurance – The part of the tax system that deals specifically with the State Pension and benefits. Broadly speaking, you pay into it when you are working, young and not in need of any benefits, and you draw from it when you are older or in need.

Net – See 'Gross' above (but take a deep breath first).

Outturn – A report or list showing the actual income and expenses of a project, or a period of time. If a budget shows the future, an outturn shows the past.

P45 – A form that a PAYE employer gives an employee if they leave during the tax year, showing how much they were paid and how much tax was deducted in that job for that year.

P60 – A form that a PAYE employer gives every employee still on their payroll at the end of the tax year, showing how much tax was deducted in that job for that year.

Partnership – A type of business shared by more than one person.

PAYE – Pay As You Earn. The tax system in the UK for most workers when they are in employment, where tax is deducted from their pay before they get it.

Payment on account – HMRC's system by which self-employed people pay some tax for the present year up front, based on their calculation for the previous year.

Probate – The process by which the estate of a deceased person is 'wound up', i.e. all their property, assets and money are assessed for tax and then distributed to whoever they have left them to.

Profit – The income of a business activity, after its expenses are deducted.

Profit and Loss statement – see also 'Outturn' – A list of all the income and expenses of a business in a given period. If there was more income than expenses, it was a profit; the other way round, it was a loss. Well done if you have spotted a logical flaw in the accounting lexicon. It should be called a Profit *or* Loss statement. Write a strongly worded letter to the Chancellor.

Quarterly update – A form sent in under the Making Tax Digital reporting system, summarising income and expenses for the past three months.

Receipt – A proof of having paid someone for something. Keep it for six years.

Self-assessment – The tax system in the UK for people who pay tax separate from or additional to PAYE.

Self-employment – Working for yourself, rather than for just one company or other person.

Shareholders – The owners of a Limited Company.

Shares – Parts or divisions of the value of a company, in the same way that slices of cake are parts or divisions of a cake (but not as tasty).

Sole trader – A self-employed person who is not in a Partnership or a Limited Company.

Subsistence – Food and drink expenses. (Sometimes people confuse this with the word 'sustenance' because of course food 'sustains' you – but the linguistic closeness is a coincidence. 'Sustenance' is not the right word to use.)

Tax code – If you work PAYE, HMRC automatically sends you and your employer a tax code. This code helps your employer to deduct the correct amount of tax from your pay. Most creatives should not worry about their tax code nor try to change it; they should look to the annual, retrospective self-assessment system to check if they have paid the correct amount of tax, and correct any mistakes at that stage.

Tax relief – A tax rebate or refund of some kind, also called a 'tax break' – a tax rule that encourages you to do something the State wants you to do (for example, to save into a pension) in return for which it lets you pay less tax. Also Theatre Tax Relief, a tax break for theatre production companies.

Tax return – A form for declaring income, expenses and tax liabilities to HMRC.

Traditional accounting – See 'accrual accounting'.

Trade – Very specifically, in your tax return, the work you were doing. This is important because you may need to distinguish between, say, your trade as an actor and your trade as a plumber. You have only one self-assessment return, but you may have two trades. (NB. You can basically do anything creative, arts or media-related within one trade.)

Tribunal – The part of the court system that hears cases and makes decisions about tax disputes.

Turnover – The total business income of a business, *before* any expenses are deducted. In effect, the same as 'sales'.

Unique Tax Reference (UTR) – A ten-digit tax reference number unique to a sole trader, Partnership or Limited Company.

VAT (Value Added Tax) – A sales tax added to many goods and services.

Zero-hours – A PAYE contract, often in a shop or catering business, where the employee is not guaranteed any hours but agrees to work on an as-and-when-needed basis.

Zzzzz – The gentle sound Alex is now making because they have finished their tax return and gone to bed.

Abbreviations

CIC A Community Interest Company

CGT Capital Gains Tax

DWP Department for Work and Pensions

HMRC His Majesty's Revenue and Customs

Ltd A Limited Company

MTD, or **MTDITSA** Making Tax Digital or, in all its glory, Making Tax Digital for Income Tax and Self-Assessment. (George Orwell said 'Never use a long word where a short one will do.' Not widely read at HMRC, our George.)

NI and **NIC** National Insurance, and National Insurance Contributions (i.e. what you pay into NI)

PAYE Pay As You Earn

PLC A Public Limited Company

QU Quarterly Update

UTR Unique Tax Reference

VAT Value Added Tax

Acknowledgements

Many people helped me greatly in this enterprise. Warm thanks in particular to my brilliant editor Sarah Lambie, and to Matt Applewhite and all the team at Nick Hern Books.

Ingrid Wassenaar (with whom I've appeared in several plays) generously and carefully read early drafts, turned my gibberish into actual English, and cut the worst jokes.

The entire team at Accounting4Actors Ltd, especially Mel Ward and Zach Collins, helped me sort the wood from the trees, and quietly picked up a lot of organisational slack while I was moonlighting to get the book done. My accounting buddies Andrew Smith, Stuart Crofton, Andie Cooley, Arron Fitzgerald, Kunal Viyala and Jon Dell know far more about tax than I will ever know and were always generous in putting me straight on my errors immediately.

Austyn Johnson of www.mortgagesforactors.com is brilliant on mortgages. Christina Poulton of www.christinapoultoncreative.co.uk is the go-to expert on company structures for creative businesses, and contributed important ideas to Chapters 6 and 7. Simon Wilson (with whom I've appeared in several plays) asked searching questions about pension provision, and Julie Stark raised some great points about allowable expenses.

All my family were amazing, especially my brother Michael who has written for many more years and with much more seriousness than I have, and gave valuable tips; and Neta Gabrieli, who patiently bore sleepless nights, early morning starts and my consequent grumpiness.

But this book would not exist in any form without my friend Tom Smith. I qualified later than many accountants do; I was the oldest person in the hall taking Finals, by some distance. One reason I was determined to finish arose from a career-crisis conversation with Tom, one day in my thirties. I'd long stopped directing, even longer stopped acting, and I wasn't getting where I wanted with producing. 'I'm just not really *good* at anything,' I wailed at him. 'Yes you are,' he said, 'You're good at explaining tax.'

www.nickhernbooks.co.uk

@nickhernbooks